DIFFERENT DRUMMERS

Also by Nell Dunn

UP THE JUNCTION   TALKING TO WOMEN   POOR COW

FREDDY GETS MARRIED (A CHILDREN'S BOOK)

THE INCURABLE   TEAR HIS HEAD OFF HIS SHOULDERS

DIFFERENT DRUMMERS

NELL DUNN

Originally published in England as *Living Like I Do*

HARCOURT BRACE JOVANOVICH   NEW YORK AND LONDON

Library of Congress Cataloging in Publication Data
Dunn, Nell, 1936–
Different drummers.
1. Single-parent family—England. 2. Collective
settlements—England. 3. Sex
customs—England. I. Title.
HQ616.D86   301.42'8   76–27413
ISBN 0–15–152928–0

First American edition

B C D E

This book is dedicated to everybody in it, with the respect I
have for those who are willing to experiment with their
domestic lives in order to find greater happiness and satisfaction
and clear the path a little for those of us who come behind.

•

It is also dedicated to my son Jem
who knows how to make life fun.

CONTENTS

1. HOW IT BEGAN 3

2. SINGLE MOTHER: JEAN AND MATTHEW 5

3. A FATHER ALONE: DAVID AND JONATHAN 13

4. A COLLECTIVE: LEEDS 17

5. NO TIES: MARY 57

6. ANARCHY : BRIGHTON 65

7. SHARING A MAN : NICOLE, JOHN AND ROSE 89

8. THE COUPLE : MARTIN AND ROSIE 99

9. A COMMUNE : RAMSGATE 105

10. LIVING WITH YOUR SISTER :
CAROLA, NICKY, IAN . . . AND ROGER 129

11. ONE HOUSE, THREE WOMEN, FOUR CHILDREN
AND THE ARTS : DINAH, ALEX AND SHEILA 141

12. BISEXUAL PARENT : JACKIE 163

13. WHAT I LEARNED 177

If a man does not keep pace with his companions,
perhaps it is because he hears a different drummer.
Let him march to the music that he hears,
however distant or far away.

HENRY DAVID THOREAU

DIFFERENT DRUMMERS

1. HOW IT BEGAN

I wanted to write a book about alternative families because of my own situation. Six years ago I separated from my husband, remaining his friend. Our three sons lived with me but spent frequent weekends and holidays with him. I was a dutiful and devoted mother, yet something wasn't working. I protected my children from my emotional problems—indeed, from all *my problems—showing them an efficient, "together" front as much as I could. This fundamental flaw in my lifestyle kept my life as a mother totally separate from my life as a woman. So much did this seem necessary that I couldn't risk caring about anyone or letting anyone share what mattered, including my everyday life— lest there be a conflict where no conflict could be tolerated.*

About a year ago I became involved with a man named Dan, who had four children. He lived alone in a ground-floor flat; his wife lived in the same house. In one way this seemed far out and ideal; in another, de-energized and static.

We spent a Christmas together in the country—me, Dan, my husband, my husband's girlfriend, Dan's wife, his wife's boyfriend and the kids. We had kippers for Christmas dinner and lots of wine—it should have been fun, but it wasn't. So I began to want to know—what are other people doing? How are my peers managing? How are people, older and younger, coping?

When the nuclear family collapses, society and the social workers are apt to think that that's the end, the children and adults are lost. This isn't true—children can and do survive outside the "family" system. And though in some ways society puts us through higher hoops and more people crash to the ground, I have also discovered that not only people with private incomes can afford to be themselves, to lead leisurely and thoughtful lives.

Domestic life is the base from which all of us operate. If we don't feel alive and free and without constraints in our domestic lives, we will never feel free outside them. Free to come and go. Free to be with our friends. Free to make love. Free to be alone.

My situation has changed since I started this book. I am now living with Dan, but we each have our own room. His four children come every other weekend and sometimes one of them stays for a week or two. Every second weekend all the children are away with their other parents. A friend, Jan, also lives in our house, and her friends from abroad call and stay. She and they are involved with our children. We share the kitchen—and food, if anyone feels like cooking—but basically, each individual, including the children, is responsible for feeding himself or herself.

There are a lot of problems, yet the density and the energy that exist with seven children and their friends in and out of the house, the different relationships and patterns that emerge, the rows between us over economics, the quarrels of the children over space and chores—all make for a life far richer than the one I had when it was me and three children on our own. **"**

The worst thing was trying to convince people that you had a child because you wanted one, and not that it was an unfortunate mistake and that you were 'so brave' and 'poor Jean'—that wasn't it at all. I was doing it solely because I wanted to do it—it was a wholly selfish gesture. I wasn't a victim—I wanted a child.

2. SINGLE MOTHER: JEAN AND MATTHEW

"Jean was twenty-two when Matthew was born. After he was born she received a degree in English from a university. There has never been a father around and perhaps this has been an advantage—Jean knew where she was from the start. Many single parents (who are single parents because of a split relationship) are in a confused position, with their children suffering from the departure of someone they love—the so-called "breakup of a family." Jean is involved more in the creation of a family, for herself and for Matthew."

WHERE FROM?

JEAN. My mother is seventy and since her children left home she has been trying to find her feet. She grew up with all the conventional expectations. Now it's hard for her to live a constructive, fulfilling life for herself because she and her peers have been appendages for so long—to husband and children—and they haven't been altogether involved in the adventure of living on a day-to-day level, like Matthew and I are. I mean, we're in it together; we're constantly remaking our world together. My parents were so fixed. It seems to me that I would find that way of life so dull, and yet people go on believing that the best setup for a family is a very fixed mother-father-child home. I know from my own mother, who had just that, that she herself has never felt fulfilled as a person. She felt she had to present to us such an anchorage of security that the obvious love between us was not enough —she had to pretend that she was wholly confident and realized in the world. She says to me, "If only I had known then what you know now."

When I first got pregnant, I was in a complex situation. Paul, my boyfriend, presumed I'd have an abortion. I was working in New York. He was American, and I couldn't get across to him that my concern wasn't with the ethics of abortion—if I wanted an abortion I'd have one—but I did think I wanted a child. The relationship, at that point, was starting to collapse and this finished it. I suddenly realized it really was me and my expanding belly and it was up to me to cope with it on my own.

In New York I was surrounded by hardheaded career people, and the pressure to have an abortion was enormous. Once I got home to England I began to feel the excitement of being pregnant—I felt a huge relief to be free and to be able to act independently. Paul stayed in New York.

I wasn't at all fearful of my position in society—I had friends who were already single parents. That made a tremendous difference. I also had very understanding parents.

The worst thing was trying to convince people that you had a child because you wanted one, and not that it was an unfortunate mistake and that you were "so brave" and "poor Jean"— that wasn't it at all. I was doing it solely because I wanted to do it—it was a wholly selfish gesture. I wasn't a victim—I wanted a child.

NOW

I lived communally with other students when I was at university, but it didn't altogether work because I was the only one who had a child. A lot of the time I found it oppressive—they were still reacting against their parents' tidy homes and flinging rubbish on the floor. So I turned into the heavy mother trying to get them to clean up. The age difference wasn't enormous; it was the experiential difference—by that time my parents were my friends, not people to be reacted against. I was more concerned with establishing some kind of loose routine so I wasn't drowned in domesticity.

At the moment I'm living next door to Ann, who also has a child on her own, and her daughter. There's lots of reciprocal baby-sitting. It's very free-flowing—if Ann has a lot to do I can take the kids off, and she'll do the same for me. But we live separate lives as adults—we've both got lots to do.

My emotional life I still find difficult. If you've summoned up the courage to tell someone you love them, then it's there, hanging in the air, the assumption—you're vulnerable—and not just you on your own but, somehow, you and the enormity of your child. Because it is an enormous weight. It's a weight I feel happy with but it's still there and perhaps that's the crux of the problem—where you don't want your potential man to feel suddenly he must become the father.

I'm glad I've gone through Matthew's preschool years financially independent. I mean, I've lived off Social Security and been continually broke but at least I've been self-supporting. I've felt far less frustrated with housewifery than a lot of my friends who are being kept have felt. This seems to be far more the problem of married couples—you make it as nice, or as chaotic, as you can cope with for yourself and your child. I'm hoping to work now that Matthew is four, but until now I've been either on a university grant or Social Security so I've been poor. . . . Poverty is not so crippling if you're not tied in a suburban situation, because the poverty is offset by the fact that you have friends around you, and fluidity of movement, because you're not married and you have less reason to shut off.

CHILDREN

It's so easy for us to feel guilty about our children—who doesn't? To feel we've just been self-indulgent and allowed ourselves all this freedom of movement and dragged the kid through it with us. But I don't think it need be like that, I don't think it is like that. In a weak moment I can feel very guilty. Why didn't I just get married and have a child? It would have been very much simpler. Yet, when I think of the realities of "getting married and having a child," I know I don't see any more real stability; the only security can be what's in oneself.

And I think when we talk of protecting our children or staying together for the sake of our children, I think it's all bullshit. Our children can accept changes. It's we who are having difficulty coming to terms with the changes, we women living without a man's support. It's less the child who is missing the father. I think children can live with tremendous fluidity, if that's the established pattern and the parent is happy with what's happening. I feel sure children need to know that there's at least one person permanently in their lives and that there will always be continuing friendships in their lives—friends whom the children know and remember—but it's we who find parting hard.

The man I lived with for two years, Phil, had been living with a woman with three children and had been oppressed with the domesticity of it all. Phil wanted me to hold Matthew back from him so he could ease in gradually, and I thought I couldn't be like that, endlessly manipulating the situation between the two of them—I've got to let them confront each other and find the area they can enjoy together. I think Matthew understood that Phil and I were deeply involved and he wanted it to be the three of us, and it never was quite like that; even after two years we never quite overcame that. I was continually being put in a position where I was being asked to choose, to choose between the responsibility and love towards Matthew and my responsibility and love for Phil. And there is no possibility of choice—you're a mother and that seems a more essential chemistry than what happens sexually between people; at least I've always found it so. Your child is there and that's absolute fact as far as I'm concerned. If you feel your child being excluded, it hurts.

I've never been married so I don't know if a woman married to the father of her children feels that same kind of friction and pressure. It wasn't that Matthew would scream every time Phil touched me or anything like that; it was much subtler. Phil was good with Matthew but he really just wanted that central, exclusive, boy-girl thing of being with me.

I was happier when I lived on my own with Matthew. At times I loved it but I could see it was a sort of dead-end street, a sort of cotton-wool world which is too protective and unreal for the child. And living with one man I found difficult because kids are pure emotion—they respond emotionally to people and they go in feet first if they like a person. This can put an enormous strain on the man, and it can put a strain on the relationship between you and the man. He is immediately swamped and it is difficult for him to form a relationship on his own terms. But I'm not prepared to interrupt whatever happens and protect the man from the child the way I've sometimes felt has been expected from me. That's something men have got to learn to cope with, too, if we're all concerned with getting more fluidity in our relationships.

A lot of men I know seem to be afraid of children—they are often self-conscious watching me at the same time as they try to interact with Matthew. So even if they're open to all the ideas, they find it hard to relate emotionally to children. It can end up with trying to keep lovers as far away as possible from Matthew. In some way men have got a lot of learning to do—or unlearn the idea that fathers are removed and mothers do all the close intimate loving. Most of the men I know are totally open to the ideas, some carry them out.

One evening Matthew said, "Do I have a daddy?" And I said, "Yes, of course you have a daddy but he lives in America." And Matthew said, "And does he know me?" And I told him, "No, because we came to England before you were born." And Matthew said, "Well, I think I ought to go and see my daddy." And he found three halfpennies for him and me and the cat to fly to America to see his daddy. Anyway, I've written to Paul and I hope he will be interested in having some kind of contact with Matthew. I'd like to demystify his image, although it's not particularly important—Matthew is interested, but not concerned.

SEX AND LOVE

My supportive relationships are often with other single parents, both in practical ways of helping each other look after each other's children and also intellectually and emotionally, having gone through a lot of the same things.

I'm increasingly tentative in my relationships with men and find myself playing the "woman with the kid who can handle her own life and doesn't need anyone, thank you very much," whereas that's not really the case—I need people and Matthew needs people.

The problem is, you want to present yourself as you are, which is an individual functioning quite happily, but on the other hand, you have a child and you don't want the man to feel either that he is excluded or that he's got to slot into some role. I wouldn't want someone to enter into a relationship with me, thinking, "O.K., she's got a child but that's nothing to do with me." He is my child and I don't want to be involved with someone who doesn't want a relationship with Matthew. And I find I have to resist saying to myself, "Oh, forget it, it's just all too complicated —it's a whole lot easier to have strings of lovers than a full relationship." But I don't want strings of lovers. I'm much more concerned with establishing a real relationship—not one with commitments for ever and ever, but one with a commitment for now.

WHERE TO

The ideal setup for me and Matthew would be to live in a large house with other people, in fairly self-contained units. For one- and two-parent families I think the nuclear family is often boring and hard work.

I do have needs as an independent woman; now Matthew will soon be going to school I am looking forward to working—to having a life outside the home. I'd like to put a lot of energy into work.

And I'd like to show Matthew that life is a very changing adventure, and not arriving in a fixed position and staying there. I'd like more children, but it seems more practical in this day and age to live with and share the care of a number of children that aren't necessarily yours.

I don't any longer assume a natural pattern, which I used to.

I remember saying to a friend when I was pregnant, "I think it will be a whole lot easier to establish relationships once I've had the baby, because he'll be there already, far easier than imagining what it might be like." But, of course, it isn't like that. That hasn't happened, although I've had a lot of good and loving relationships. Now Matthew is four years old and I've come to terms with the fact that it's never going to be that simple. I grew up in a very secure environment and somehow I just expected the same thing to happen to me. Now I know it's always going to be different. But I don't think my difficulties are any greater than the average suburban housewife's difficulties, probably much less. In a way she has so many fewer options than me—at least I have all possibilities open to me and I assume I'll go on making relationships that mean a lot to me. But I don't presume that I'm going to find the one that's going to mean everything to me forever. My life's always been in a state of flux, ever since I was eighteen years old, and I think our children will come to terms with flux and change more easily than us—Matthew is excited at the prospect of new things rather than frightened of them.

Jean talks about the difficulty of lovers establishing a relationship with a child who isn't theirs. I feel the situation is different in marriage but not necessarily easier.

In a nuclear family, apart from the dullness Jean talks about, there can be endless tensions as child competes with child or parent for attention. It occurs to me that many married parents resolve this by becoming a sort of business partnership, the "business" being running a home and bringing up children. And with the setting up of the business, romantic and erotic love disappear. There's no room for it; it's distracting to a well-run institution.

Jean and Matthew dispel a myth—you don't need marriage, or even money, to create a happy child. Matthew is beautiful, his life is rich. All you need is a lot of courage and energy.

> *I kept him, one, because I was learning to love him; two,*
> *because I didn't know what else to do with him; three, be-*
> *cause I felt my parents wanted me to.*

3. A FATHER ALONE:
DAVID AND JONATHAN

'*David has brought up his son Jonathan since he, David, was
twenty. His wife (finding motherhood too much for her) often
said, "Either he goes or I go." One day she went, taking Jonathan.
A month later she returned him.*

*David and Jonathan (a tiny baby) went to live with David's
parents because he said, "I simply didn't know what to do
next." When Jonathan was four his grandmother died.*

*Jonathan is now ten and lives with his father, who works in an
art foundry, and his father's girlfriend. Each morning they go
together on the bus—David gets off at his work stop and Jonathan
goes on to school. In the evenings David collects Jonathan from
his grandfather's house and takes him home.*'

A FATHER

DAVID. I kept him, one, because I was learning to love him; two, because I didn't know what else to do with him; three, because I felt my parents wanted me to.

I got great pleasure from the physical side of caring for him—changing diapers and washing diapers I thoroughly enjoyed. A baby's shit has a fresh, primitive smell about it. I like the domestic side of life.

I think, when I'm feeling warm within myself, I can have a clear relationship with my child; but when I'm feeling unsure, then a relationship with a child is very confusing. Perhaps to be near anybody, but especially a child, is difficult if you can't get on with him on a straightforward level.

He was at a state day nursery until he was five. I'd fetch him after work, take him home, feed him, then, depending on how I felt and he behaved, either loved him or hated him. Then eventually I'd put him to bed. Next morning I'd take him to the nursery again.

I found it easy to chat up women because they were intrigued by the fact that I was bringing up a child—it held a magic for them. I didn't wish to develop relationships with women at that time; I found them very frightening, so Jonathan was very useful. I used to say, "I've got to go home and look after my son," or, "I'm sorry, I can't make love to you, I'm worried about Jonathan." I used to use him as an excuse for situations. Even if he was with friends, I could never stay the night with a woman —Jonathan was a very good excuse and I'd have to get up halfway through the night and go home.

I did live for a while with a woman who had a child of Jonathan's age. We met at the nursery. It didn't work because I couldn't cope with the frictions and jealousies that arose between the boys and between myself and the woman. It should have worked but it didn't. But Jonathan still misses Michael as he might a brother.

I'm now living with Sue, who has no children, and is older than myself. It was difficult at first. She wasn't used to children; she was frightened of them and I myself didn't feel very confident as a father. Sue and I are still learning how to live together. It is difficult. There are moments of joy and depths of sadness, feelings of exaltation and moods of depression—and moments of despair; occasionally peace.

The school holidays are awful. I used to lie awake (I still do) a few nights before the school holidays, worrying about what to do with my son. There were play centers open but I found it difficult to find anyone who would take him. I began work at eight in the morning and most play centers didn't open until nine. I found it difficult to get regular help from anyone—everyone had some excuse. The reason I had to get someone else to take him was that I was too scared to take the time off work to take him myself. If I couldn't get anyone then he had to stay at home all day long playing round the house. I'd go home at lunchtime and cook him up some soup. Even now I find holidays a great worry —I've found them the most difficult part of not being married. I just view them with a great big W—Worry, that's what they mean. Christmas is coming up now and I'm beginning to worry about that. I found it worst when he first started school, between five and eight. The day nursery didn't have any holidays. Now he's a bit more independent.

I feel one effect of his not having had a mother is that it's made him frightened of women, though in their company he pretends to be quite confident. He's only spoken about his own mother a couple of times and that in a very cagey way, as if he were in no-man's-land. I think he has a lot of reservations in the direction of women, although he and Sue have now become friends.

The older he gets the more embarrassed he gets about physical affection. I love holding him and kissing him and cuddling him.

Up until about a month ago I used to kiss him every morning before I got off the bus and he went on to school. Now he gets embarrassed so we've stopped it.

Sometimes he gets very miserable without really knowing why.

It's been a struggle, there have been moments of pleasure and enlightenment. I get a deep pleasure out of children's company, I enjoy talking to them. I love my son very much, I'd miss him if he went . . . very much.

I think bringing him up has been the most creative thing I've done, creative in the sense of helping another being grow up.

I feel very moved by the tenderness children show towards their parents, and the tenderness that can be returned. I feel that tenderness can only come from a creative instinct to build something between you. But although there are these beautiful moments, I don't think one can evade the fact that it's often a very annoying and difficult job.

In the morning, you kiss your child good-bye, you look in each other's eyes and you smile—he goes on his way and you go on yours. But that isn't all there is to it. I wouldn't like to have to go through it again.

People say to me, "If you're in a good situation with a woman and you have a child, then there's two of your bringing him up," but I don't think I could trust a woman deeply enough. Perhaps I could with the woman I'm now living with. . . . I feel she is of the earth . . . with her I'd like to blossom.

David and Jonathan show that men can bring up children without women. But I couldn't help thinking that life might have been much easier for David had he been part of a collective like the Leeds parents, whose story follows.

Nearly everyone had had a sexual relationship with everyone else in the collective at one time or another, except the men with each other. There appeared to be no censoriousness about each other's lives both in the sex and work ethics—people slept with whom they liked and worked when *they liked—but complete responsibility was expected about those things that were agreed on, such as house chores and child care.*

4. A COLLECTIVE: LEEDS

On my first visit I stayed in Abbey Road.

When I arrived they'd all gone to a play in a local pub—A Woman's Work is Never Done. *A note had been left saying there was some supper in the oven. I was hungry so I opened a big bottle of white wine I'd bought on my way from the station, using a corkscrew on the side of a small can opener, got the vegetable pie out of the oven and sat at the kitchen table on a chair next to the cat in front of the portable heater.*

Then I opened the back door from the kitchen. It goes almost straight into a little back street joined by an alley. I saw a fat black woman with a knitted blue hat sewn with silver sequins go into the house opposite.

It is a corner house. All the rooms are odd shapes, walls painted different colors, floorboards old, doors yellow, bright linoleum, tin plates above the sink.

After the theater they came back—Lisa, Tony, Annie and Albert. We sat on cushions on the floor of the living room in front of the fire and drank the rest of my wine.

I slept in Alex's room because Alex was in the hospital with an abscess. Bed on floor, electric heater, very tidy, with loads of pamphlets on such subjects as gay lib. Noise of music from other houses. Bright shirts hanging over the bookshelves. Written on the door: "Survival without a wage is a full-time occupation."

How the Leeds Collective Works. *Everyone has a room of his own. There are four houses, all within walking distance of each other. Abbey Road, where Lisa, Annie, Alex, Albert and Tony live (and where Jan used to live); Penny Lane, where Tom, Una, Jenny and George live; Greystone Road, where Carol and her two boys Brian (nine years old) and Sean (seven) live in public housing. And then, new on the scene, Jan's flat, where Jan lives. Sylvia is somewhat "floating." George, forty, is on a sabbatical from teaching at Sydney University. The children—Sam (who is two and one-half, biological mother Jan), Hannah (two and one-half, biological parents Una and Tom), Gill (two and one-half, biological mother Sylvia) and Misha (one and one-half, biological mother Annie)—move in turn among the houses. (Carol's sons, Brian and Sean are only on this rota at weekends and Misha spends about two days a week at another house altogether, two miles away. While she's there she joins in another collective child-care setup similar to this one.) Only two children sleep in one house on any night but all spend the days together. Getting the children up and all the chores are shared by the grown-ups. There is a list stuck up in the kitchen so everyone knows where the kids are and whose turn it is to do all the various jobs. These schedules are worked out at the house meeting and the weekly crèche meeting to fit in with each person's individual life and plans. If one person is doing a full-time job then he mightn't*

*have a crèche day but instead would do more of getting the
children up and putting them to bed. During the day there are
always two people looking after the children.*

*On the surface this looks rigid but, in fact, the children's lives
are very informal. They join in supper at whichever house they
are sleeping in and romp about afterwards and get played with
and talked to and finally put to bed. It is much as in any family
except that it is probably more interesting—there is more happening, more people are about and the evening life is not dominated
by television but rather by music and talk. They don't have a lot
of toys but a lot of people instead.*

*They lead full, active lives. They go to a play group three times
a week and the rest of the time have each other to play with.
I felt when I was there that they had a lot of people very interested in them—they were both talked to and talked about a great
deal. If they lack anything it is solitariness, that still and private
time I remember as a child.*

*Financial arrangements vary from house to house. At Abbey
Road money is shared as nearly as possible, with all incomes
pooled and, after the bills are paid, the remainder divided. At
Penny Lane, everyone shares bills but keeps his own money for
himself.*

*When Carol and Jan had their own places they were independent
financially. Now Carol and Jan are about to move in together,
making only three establishments in the collective.*

*Nearly everyone had had a sexual relationship with everyone
else in the collective at one time or another, except the men with
each other. There appeared to be no censoriousness about each
other's lives both in the sex and work ethics—people slept with
whom they liked and worked when they liked but complete responsibility was expected about those things that were agreed on,
such as house chores and child care.*

•

*On my second visit to Leeds, I stayed in Penny Lane and read
"The Crèche Book." The crèche book moved around with the
children, ostensibly so anyone could write down what was hap-*

pening—if, for example, a child had a cold or wouldn't walk to the park—so as to get some consistency. There were some good lists of words: penis—willy; vagina—gina; clitoris—clit. Quite a lot else got expressed in the book, like anger over Sam's being shut in his room till he had put his socks on and if the last person had left the "kid's room like a shithouse." It seemed quite a good way of people keeping in touch with one another's irritations and ideas.

Later I went for a walk through Meanwood (the next neighborhood) with Tom, down footpaths along the backs of Edwardian suburban houses. We passed gardens, goats, a suckling foal, garages homemade of wood and corrugated iron. Past peonies, hollyhocks and—something wartime about it—hens clucking and a man mending a black Austin Prefect.

I liked the ease and grace with which the men handled the children, the cooking, the domestic scenes. For them there was no mystique about the "woman's role" and therefore immediately I found it easier to relate—the range was wider—we talked as people. How often in my life I have felt a constraint with men who weren't in any definite role of either a lover or work colleague. As if the only way to talk was in terms of what they did, "plumber" or "lawyer," or as someone else's "lover" or "husband." Here there was little or no constraint and I continually came upon little happenings like Una and Jenny, both naked, bending over the bath while Jenny washed Una's hair.

In the evening Tina and I went to Jan's party. It was all for the women's movement and there were no men. Beautiful women danced together and lounged about, kissing, holding hands, talking, smoking, drinking, and I have to admit I got a big kick watching the women having such a good time without men. **99**

WHERE FROM?

TOM is twenty-nine.

I was living with my wife, Una, and our baby, Hannah, and we thought the physical structure was much too limited. It was claustrophobic, it was inadequate, it just wasn't enough.

We thought the idea of mother-love was overemphasized and that the one-mummy–one-daddy setup made the parents overdependent on the child and the child overdependent on the parents. It also placed too much strain on the parents to give the child everything.

We came across the Abbey Road collective and we started some kind of communal child-care and that involved us with other adults. And so relationships between the various adults began and gradually it turned into what we have now, which is a collective upbringing for the kids. Una and I also thought it would help our relationship sort itself out.

UNA is twenty-six.

Before Hannah was born, Tom and I had a very good relationship. We were always doing crazy, spontaneous things. I was very active when I was pregnant. I did a degree and I bicycled a lot and had a lot of fun.

Then Hannah was a very bad birth. Everything went wrong and after the birth I went really downhill. I got prolapsed ovaries and I was exhausted and became very dependent on Tom and I got very frustrated—I thought, I've been through all this and look now! This went on for a year—I wanted to do nothing but sleep. If we'd been living in a collective situation this would never have happened. I became very cold and lost all interest in sex.

I found married life incredibly frustrating because before that I was at university and had been relatively free, and then suddenly, having a child, I had to cut down on so many activities. Tom went out to work and I stayed home looking after Hannah. My whole day was a routine and I had this guilt feeling that I ought to be much more active with her and be doing things all the time; but I found I got very lethargic—I didn't even read or feel like doing anything creative.

When we came to Leeds I put Hannah in a nursery so I could do a teacher-training course, and I felt guilty about this because it wasn't a very good nursery. Then, when we came home in the evenings, it was like an anticlimax. Hannah obviously hated the nursery and was difficult. I felt constantly guilty and yet I needed to do this course in case I needed to get a job.

I think it destroyed the relationship between Tom and me; I became quite frigid. Then we met up with Abbey Road and slowly the idea of us joining the collective was realized. By that time it seemed too late to salvage our marriage. I joined the women's group and began to make friends.

JENNY is twenty-five.

I was in Leeds living with a guy and wanting to leave him. But I had no friends of my own, didn't really know where to go. I was very dependent. Then I joined the women's movement eighteen months ago. I was dissatisfied with my situation but I tended to think it was because I'd failed. Meeting and talking to a whole group of women who were experiencing just the same kinds of frustrations in their lives stopped me thinking I was some kind of freak. It's realizing you're not alone which is the best thing about it.

I met some people here and moved in.

SYLVIA is twenty-six.

I've lived in so many different situations that I don't seem to be able to find my actual "destination," and at present I am not quite certain where I wish to belong.

LISA is twenty-eight.

I found it was horrible living in a couple situation. I was more lonely then than I've ever been in my life before or since. When I was a student I was living in a flat and there was loads going on and Tony moved in. Then we both left university in nineteen sixty-nine. We went to live in Oxford and it was a horrible shock because we were sharing a flat and I got a job but I didn't meet anyone I could relate to at work. And it was just really lonely.

People think you're self-sufficient as a couple and that you don't want anyone to talk to when you're living together. So I got so I couldn't imagine going out without Tony. If someone asked me out I'd say, "Well, can I bring Tony, too?" thinking, well, he lives this boring life and I've had this exciting invitation so I've got to bring him along, too. So of course that made it much worse. It was really bad and we were saved because Tony rejoined the political group he was in before and I joined a women's group and started to get my own friends. We'd always had friends only as a couple and I would never have visited them on my own. Then the women's group opened things up for me.

Tony and I had been completely monogamous for two and a half years—not by intent but just because it happened that way and we were living in one room with one bed. Then we went to a party and I got off with Alex, and Tony got off with a woman, and that was the end of monogamy. But there was no hassle about it because we were both so sick of the whole thing. We went on living in one room and talking about everything that happened.

Soon after that we started a food collective, which I see as the real beginning of everything. We all lived within five minutes of each other, so we all cooked in rota—it was six men and me, which I didn't much like.

That went on for nearly two years in Oxford. Slowly, more and more people joined, so in the end there were sixteen of us and we ate in two different houses each night. We used to draw names out of a hat each week to see where we'd eat—it was a fluctuating thing with people coming and going.

Out of that grew a kind of group sex scene. Looking back, it seems horrific but at the time I suppose we were experimenting in free sexuality—you weren't meant to mind who you slept with, or who was in the room. That created quite a lot of resentments. I certainly wouldn't do it now—I feel so much calmer about my sexuality—it was a whole lot of throwing off conditioning. At that time sex was a big thing and sex and relationships everything. We were also involved in campaigns like squatting [taking over a house that is empty and paying no rent] and the women's group.

Then Jan came along in the summer of seventy-two. She'd got pregnant and was no longer with the guy. I'd always been very against having kids—because I saw them as a drag and because I would have to stop working. Then I got to know these people in London and they were bringing up kids collectively and it seemed marvelous and I couldn't imagine doing it any other way. Jan said she wanted to bring up her kid collectively, so that's what we decided to do. It began to seem very important that a kid should be brought up to relate to more than one person and we hoped the idea would spread.

TONY is twenty-six.

I grew up in a straight middle-class family in Essex, but I was encouraged to learn to cook and sew and I never balked at any so-called women's jobs.

I met Lisa at Durham University and after our finals we went to live in Oxford together. Later Alex joined us and then Jan.

In Oxford we had a much wider, looser collective based around having an evening meal. There were about twelve of us who used to eat together from three different households, taking it in turns to cook without really working out why we were doing it. People slept with each other quite a bit—we had very little space and it was very chaotic. It was an important time for me, and the three of us—Alex, Lisa and myself—put a lot of energy into it.

ALEX is thirty.

When I was about sixteen I started reading Reich, and when I went to university I got involved in this Bohemian libertarian group that was going on; and one of the features of that group was that there were a lot of women who, in the parlance of the time, were seen as "emancipated" women. I remember there was this woman, Ena, who, the first time I met her, got out her diaphragm and explained contraception to me. So most of my early sexual experience was with very confident, aware women. Several years later I had a couple relationship for two years. But once we started getting into the structure of living together and being responsible for each other's emotions, it started to get very tense and she clung on even more. So by the time I'd met Tony and

Lisa I'd found out by first-hand experience I didn't want that sort of close couple relationship or anything to do with it again.

I started a scene with Lisa and at first Tony was very threatened. But out of a variety of reasons we stayed together and worked through a lot of Tony feeling very jealous of me sleeping with Lisa and then later my jealousy over Lisa sleeping with Tony. The reasons we decided to work through it all together lay in the wider social, cultural and political events going on at that time: the early flowering of the women's liberation movement; the resurgence of militant grass-roots politics in the community, outside both workplaces and universities; the fusion between left-wing politics and the "counterculture" of rock, dope and experimentation. In our household we were becoming aware of the politics of everyday life and realizing that *all* aspects of the way people live, including things as prosaic as cooking or as private as sex, have political implications.

JAN is twenty-three.

You see, ever since I was pregnant I lived with the Abbey Road lot, Lisa and Alex and Tony. Sam was born with them—that is the family he was born into. I married Sam's father when I was eighteen but we split up when I was pregnant. I still enjoy seeing him from time to time but I don't think we could live together.

I met him when I was hitching—he gave me a lift.

ALBERT is twenty-one.

I was teaching at the Free School and I went on the Free School camp and I met Lisa. So I came into the house via my relationship with Lisa in November of seventy-four, when I was twenty.

The crèche was the thing I liked the best. I have four brothers and four sisters in the nuclear family setup, which I didn't like. But I like kids and wanted to live with them.

My background is Leeds working class. My father was violent and often beat us, and my mother took one side and then the other. One minute she'd be stopping our father hitting us, the next minute she'd be saying we'd done this or that and should be hit. She had to go out cleaning to earn money which was taken away by my father. I suppose I came from a deprived working-class nuclear family.

ANNIE is twenty-five.

I moved up north and ended up in Leeds, living with a lot of people in the drug scene. At first I liked this—I was part of a group and I felt less of a freak. They were passive, quiet people, a lot of semimusicians. The women were expected to be Earth Mothers—to make herb tea and read religious books and cook enormous quantities of cheap food. And it was very squalid.

It was a dual thing; you're respected as a woman and at the same time you're shat on. None of the men were working, so to maintain their position as men, they had to be heavier than usual and really shitty. All the women I knew didn't use contraception—they all had babies. Women were stereotyped in the mother (the Virgin Mary sort of mother) and the whore who was on the pill and everyone looked down on her. It's a very sad scene. The women have a very low opinion of themselves; they're very passive and very dependent on their men.

Anyway, finally I got pregnant, perhaps partly because I wanted to show my parents I could be a mother.

I met the Abbey Road people because I was taken to court for squatting and they are into helping people over legal hassles. I was pregnant, fed up with S, so I came to live in Abbey Road. At first I was uneasy because they were much more educated, academic and together than I was and I didn't know anything about women's liberation or politics.

They had been thinking about adopting a kid because at the time they had only Sam. So I decided to have Misha born into the collective. We gave her the name of Misha Wild because Sam is called Sam Wild, so they both have the same surname. And now I'm glad and I wouldn't want to have her any other way.

Then I went to a women's movement camp. It was the first time I'd ever been with all women and I thought, "Wow! This is great!"

CAROL is twenty-nine.

When I lived with the kids on my own I built this cocoon around us. A divorcée is a put-down status in England. If you go to someone's house they tend to lock their husbands away—as soon as I was divorced a lot of my friends stopped asking me round. I thought, Well this is my burden, I'd better just get on with it!

The pattern was myself and the children, the children and myself—there was no one else. Then the various people in the collective said they'd like to take Brian and Sean out, and it was a shock that anyone should want to. It was the first time that anyone had offered to take my kids out. Then the kids started visiting them on their own and sometimes staying the night, and if we went anywhere they'd want to send cards back to them.

NOW

TONY.   When we moved to Leeds we established this thing of each having a room to ourselves. I have heard of collectives where having your own room was considered to be petty bourgeois privatization and they even drew lots to see who would sleep with who.

TOM.   It's affected my relationship with Una in various ways, mostly, perhaps, because of the sexual relationships within the collective. I've got involved with different people—I think Una's and my relationship had to change anyway and all this did was accelerate the process.

Relationships here tend to be more open-ended; that kind of intimate, committed relationship takes time and hasn't really happened for me with anyone else. Perhaps this is a transition stage and is inevitable in this kind of setup.

We try to live out our political ideas. In a sense, Una and I have gone past the point of choice—we can't get a divorce and fight over Hannah in the conventional way. There are lots of other people involved, and Sam, Gill and Misha are like Hannah's brother and sisters; it would be difficult to take her away.

TONY. I've been through phases of being isolated, but as to my relationship with Lisa it's gone on so long and there are so many aspects to it that I can't see how it could stop.

I get most uptight with the men in the house—we try to talk things out. Occasionally there are physical fights—Lisa, me and Albert have had a few physical fights. I was very tense at the time and he was nagging me over household chores and it blew up into a manic row. I felt very remorseful about hurting him.

ANNIE. My close relationships in the household change all the time. I've gone through some really bad times of not getting on at all with just about everybody in the collective at one time or another. I've freaked out and considered leaving but really I accept that as part of living collectively—for me, it's bound up with living in a city. If I lived in the country I could go through very bad things with people and then go for a walk and get a whole lot of space and I'd come back and feel much better and stronger, but that's impossible in Leeds. Sometimes here I feel it's just one hassle after another and what's the point? You get over one and then there's hardly breathing space before another begins, but I think if I was living somewhere with more trees and stuff I could get over it better and it wouldn't feel like that. I don't think any of the problems are insoluble and I don't think any of the people I live with are awful, but sometimes everything seems like that.

LISA. I run a women's health course, covering such things as contraception, childbirth, abortion, menopause and mental health. But I can't earn enough to keep myself on that so I have to do jobs like modeling as well.

My aim is to live out the kind of lifestyle I preach but I think I'm very lucky to have that amount of purity. It's taken a long time setting it up and we are always a bit broke. It's a constant battle for survival, when you just don't want to think about money. I used to get very envious of the unsupported biological mothers who have a regular income from Social Security for sixteen years—and they're doing the same amount of child-care that I am, and I have to go out and do modeling for money. I don't feel money ought to be a big thing but it really is when you haven't got it.

UNA. At first I didn't trust everyone, but now—because I know everyone well—I trust everybody. I feel equally warmly towards the four children, and I would be extremely unhappy were I to be separated from any of them.

I never yearn for the closed family unit of me, Tom and Hannah. Now we live in the house together we see each other a lot. In a way, I'd like to have a scene with Tom but I'm frightened of it slipping back into what it was and us starting to abuse one another.

The women seem to get a lot of support from among themselves and the men don't—the men turn to the women, too.

Sharing money is the easiest part of the whole thing. We do have arguments about cleaning up but we've learnt to cope with that. My criteria are: I want the kitchen very clean out of hygienic reasons, but the rest of the house I don't mind about too much.

There has been difficulty because some people are working and have more money than those on Social Security; but then the ones on Social Security have the advantage of structuring their lives and the possibility of working in less alienated set-ups. We want to sort it out so that we all take it in turns to work.

I feel I'm learning to be more sensitive, that people do have different needs, that people are different and that all of us have good and bad qualities and there is so much to discover.

I think it's important that the collective doesn't close its doors to the outside world. We can be a bit forbidding to an individual—some people are threatened by an idea—and our children are scrutinized more than most.

ANNIE. Two years ago I was like a freak. I didn't care about my clothes, I didn't want to work; I wanted to live in the country, smoke dope, have kids and sew. I wanted to be constructive but I didn't know in what. Now I've plenty of opportunity to be constructive, both politically active and looking after the kids, the play group et cetera. It's a matter of deciding just what I want to do. I get very confused about things still, about to what extent I should push myself to do things I find hard, or if I should just drift along.

ALBERT. Twice I've had physical fights with the two of them—once because I missed my turn to cook. I back out at violence, because I've seen too much in my past. Lisa can get really angry with me and hit me hard enough to bruise me, but because I'm against violence I don't feel I can hit her back. I get jealous of the way Tony always takes her side.

Always, where I've lived before, I've cooked sausage, eggs and chips, and other greasy foods. When I moved in and I was asked to take my place in the cooking schedule, I didn't even know how to boil potatoes—I could chip them but not boil them, and I'd never cooked vegetables. I got into watching people cook and that's how I learnt. And then I began to look in recipe books and started to really enjoy cooking.

SYLVIA. I've never felt before that I'm enclosing myself in such a nutshell . . .

I think it's a positive thing for Gill, a good thing. Most communes I've lived in just want to smoke dope all the time and avoid any responsibility, but here everyone cares a lot for the kids.

But a lot of my enthusiasm for communal living has gone— I don't feel accepted here. Gill has been accepted and has grown fond of the other children, and I couldn't possibly take her away with me. I can't expect to structure a life for a child on my own.

I would have preferred to have had a deep relationship with some of the women here, and I tried. But lots of times when I tried to get to know them, they've rejected me, so I've become passive and apathetic.

TONY. I've felt slightly pissed off with Jan over her change of heart, that she is considering taking Sam out of the collective. I think if she did take Sam off on her own she'd have to change her lifestyle a lot in ways she doesn't realize. There is a very practical side to collective child-care which is the sharing of the shit work. But I hope we'll be able to talk it out.

We had a fairly exclusive relationship when she was living here in Abbey Road. When she was pregnant she needed lots of physical and emotional support; I found the relationship good for me, and that set the tone. I partly wanted, and partly felt obliged, to stick to her through thick and thin, and that structured our relationship till well after we moved to Leeds—though I did have other hetero- and homosexual relationships. I wanted to live my own life, so in the end Jan got pissed off and chose to wash her hands of the relationship.

JAN. I think I was inconsistent when I was living in the commune at Abbey Road. I think of them as five individuals. There is a lot about me which is different and a disappointment to the others.

I used to believe that one could forget one's roots and wipe them out and they wouldn't matter. I'm not so sure these days.

I've lived collectively for the last three or four years and I needed to leave, to have a place of my own where I could piece myself together and see what I want out of life. And I really want to live by myself. My friend, Diane, lives nearby but not with me. It's the first time I've had a place to myself. I went to a boarding school until I was eighteen.

I find money really hard—it's much cheaper, in terms of buying food et cetera, collectively. I find managing to live really hard and that's been a big divider lately between me and the rest.

CAROL. I don't find it too tough being on my own now. It was such a relief getting out of a bad marriage. I've got people now that I can call on if I need help, and people to discuss the kids with— so I'm not strictly on my own. Though I wouldn't want to live in one of the communal houses—I value my privacy. I don't mind people staying here for periods of time, but the idea of someone living here would drive me insane. I've got my own way of doing things; it's a whole lifestyle and I couldn't change it and I don't want to. I've got a perfect setup here; I've no reason to change it. Perhaps I'm too selfish to live in a collective situation. I don't think you have to live in a communal house to have freedom; I've got an awful lot of freedom now.

It's made an enormous difference to me—every other weekend I have a weekend free. I don't have to worry about the kids; I know they're being well looked after. I look forward to these weekends by myself. The first couple of times I was wandering around from Friday to Monday wondering what on earth to do with myself. I was just hanging around and then I said, This is ridiculous, you've got all this time and you're just not doing anything with it. Now I've got used to it I do all sorts of things, any amount of things. Don't ask me what but anyway, I have a nice time.

The children want to go. They know where they're going for the weekend and they really look forward to the change of scene. Also, the weekends I spend with the children I enjoy and I plan to do things with them, and they enjoy the babies.

CHILDREN

UNA. I appreciate most here that I can trust people with the children and that I have so much freedom, that I can take a job without having to put my child in an awful nursery.

I am so pleased that she has sisters and a brother without me having to provide them. I have a close friend who is in a married situation with three children. I see myself as having a much freer life than her and I feel no envy for her marriage, though it seems a good marriage.

ALBERT. The kids here have much more freedom. They are related to as people, which I never was, and the way they move around to different houses I really like. They get so many chances of different experiences, whereas I only saw the inside of one miserable house.

I feel very close to the kids here, not as a father, but as a friend. I really enjoy their company. I get freaked by Jan wanting to take Sam away. That's a big disadvantage, this insecurity because Jan is his biological mother. It feels as if she can take my kid away.

I've been doing three crèche days a week at the moment because Tony is doing his exams and Annie and George are in Portugal. I feel I should do less household chores, but people still get on my back about it.

We don't give our children sweets for health reasons, and when Jan gives Sam sweets I feel furious. So it isn't always easy to get consistency, which is upsetting.

LISA. I never realized how difficult it would be dealing with small kids but I get a hell of a lot out of it. I'd hate to do it full time, but one day a week we plan what we're going to do and do it and it's pretty nice. I don't want a child of my own—there are so many kids around who need time and attention. Also, I hate the idea of being pregnant—it makes me feel sick. I had an abortion last summer—I felt there was this horrible parasite inside me and it was a great relief to have an abortion. I felt, now my body can go back to normal and belong to me again.

Often there are difficulties between, perhaps, two of the adults but, as there are so many other people, it needn't affect the kids. Unlike in a nuclear family, the tensions here can be absorbed.

UNA. Sometimes I have felt cross that things were inconsistent. Just having a collective situation I don't think is enough—you need to continually talk about it and get a consistent method. So there has been an enormous amount to talk through—things like whether Misha, at one year old, should have a bottle or not. I feel I had contributions to make but I also learned a lot. From Lisa I learned that kids were people—something I hadn't thought much about. She would talk to them and get them to dress themselves (even Misha partly dresses herself) and just treated them as people.

I don't feel I've lost my role of "mother" because I feel I'm mother to four instead. What I had before I wasn't enjoying. When I had to stay day after day with Hannah I lost my temper. When she was crying I'd put her to bed. Perhaps she was crying because she was bored, and I was bored, too. Now I'm pleased to be with the kids and I put a lot into it. That didn't come straightaway—at first I was watching Hannah all the time and wondering if I was doing the right thing or fucking up her life. Then I decided if I was going to do it, I might as well put my whole self into it.

ANNIE. Sometimes I feel I haven't any relationship with Misha at all. I've just come back from Portugal so I haven't seen her for three weeks. I completely entrust her to other people. When I was in Lisbon I saw, in a shop, some tiny shoes, really beautiful little shoes, and I suddenly got this feeling of love and longing to see the kids—not just Misha but all of them—and I felt really upset for about two hours. Yet I know so well I can trust everyone here to take care of them.

Early on, when she was born, I breast-fed her for two weeks, but I didn't like doing it, I felt so anxious all the time. When she was six months old she used to scream a lot and Lisa would get very uptight with her and they'd battle together—Lisa getting angry with Misha and Misha with Lisa—and that used to upset me. I never interfered but it used to upset me. But I still agree on the principle that people must work out their own relationships, and now Misha and Lisa get on O.K. For quite a while I felt Lisa was cold with the kids, but I felt I had renounced being Misha's mother so I couldn't, or shouldn't, compensate. But at the same time I felt regret that Misha was missing out on the warmth I thought she ought to have.

For the first two months after she was born I was continually paranoid, postnatal depressed and full of mixed-up mother feelings. It was horrible, but after that I switched off and didn't want anything to do with her for quite a while. I think I've consciously avoided making a mother-bond with her so that other people can have an equal link with her. I feel differently about her—it's not that I care more for her, it's just that I feel differently about her.

I don't think my relationship with her is very important. I can see how together she is and I feel no anxiety about her. I've decided I'm not going to worry about her, I'm just going to let her get on with things and she does and she's fine. I'm not necessary to her as an individual, I feel the love I can give the other kids is a very pure love, it's not egotistical when it's not your own kid. My feelings for Sam, Gill and Hannah are better feelings because they are related to them as people and not as a possession or extension of myself.

TONY. The main difference here is I've got involved with children that I wasn't biologically responsible for. It seemed a fairly natural process—inasmuch as I was having a relationship with Jan, who was pregnant with Sam when I met her—and I suppose I did adopt a slightly fatherly role when Sam arrived. I felt I wasn't a teenager anymore, that I had responsibilities. I am incredibly fond of them—I'm particularly attached to Sam and to Misha, too. Gill and Hannah, I'm fond of them as well but I feel slightly less bound up with them, whereas I feel my life will be forever bound up with Sam and Misha.

I don't feel a desire for a biological child of my own—I'd rather see this collective work as it is, rather than have too many children around.

ALEX. When we first started there was an ideology of not believing in possessive relationships and not treating the kids as objects. And right now the whole issue of adult control is coming up over Jan and Sam, and it's almost swung to the opposite extreme. There's something in the way you relate to a child who's dependent on you that isn't like an autonomous adult, so it's much more difficult to work out things about possessiveness. I'm against it but you have to take up a responsible attitude—you can't just say "You go your way and I'll go mine," like you can to another grown-up.

You really have to cooperate with each other on a very committed level. I got very freaked out about it because, as I'm not biologically connected to any child and also I'm a man, the fact that I've been involved with Sam from before he was born and love him a lot more—in the eyes of society that doesn't count.

When Jan said she felt maternal to Sam, I felt a lot of outsiders gave her their support because she's the mother. And I felt, if I'd moved out and then come along to a crèche meeting (like Jan did) and said, "I want more of Sam, I want him to be based at my place," then people wouldn't have thought I had any right about it because I wasn't his mother. They'd just have said, "Oh, Alex must be freaking." Sam has heard kids at the play group saying "Mummy," so sometimes he uses it to call me or Tony or anyone else in this house. I hope when he goes to school he'll be able to say, "I've got five mummies and four daddies."

CAROL. The crèche has been very good for Brian and Sean. It's taught them to relate to other people. Up to a couple of years ago they only knew me—their father disappeared seven years ago and we haven't heard from him since. Now they have other adults they can talk to and stay the night with. They like staying the night away from me and I like staying the night away from them.

JENNY. We have a crèche meeting here once a week and we discuss everything to do with the children. For instance, Sam used to refuse to walk—he'd lie in the road screaming "Carry! Carry!" So we had to discuss what to do in order to get consistency. When Gill was having all her tantrums we discussed that a lot and got Sylvia to tell us all about what had happened to her in the past —which was a help.

ALEX. The kids don't seem to have much trouble in adjusting to sleeping in different houses. Misha never seems to wake at night and the others rarely do.

UNA. We try and get our children to walk a lot—they never go in strollers—and now they're very good at walking.

I am glad that I'm a mother and have gone through being pregnant and giving birth. For me it has been a very valuable experience, but I don't really want any more children because I have these four.

JENNY. Lisa brought it up in the crèche book—did the biological parents feel more secure than the nonbiological parents? In other words, a biological parent could emigrate any time with a child. On the other hand, as someone pointed out, a nonbiological parent could say, "Well, bugger your crèche," and leave the biological parents back in the nuclear thing.

TOM. With collective child-care the men and the women take equal part, which means the children don't get stereotyped roles of mummy doing the women's things and daddy playing football for half an hour after tea. In some senses what we're doing is breaking down the biological ties, which involves problems. It's a big responsibility and I do have doubts. Having said that, I'll say I don't necessarily think biological ties are that important.

Also, because of our situation when Una and I were a nuclear family, child-care often seemed a chore. I would get pissed off and irritated with Hannah because she was there twenty-four hours a day. Now it is a positive pleasure to see her.

People often try to fulfill themselves through their children, and there is pressure on the child to shine for mummy and daddy. I think collective child-care avoids this—the parents can't live through their children, you don't have the domestic womb to fall back on. It's become a more fluid thing and you're forced back on yourself, and that involves change and adaptation that has to take place. I've found in black times I can no longer lean against my wife and child. I have to prop myself up, which is a good thing but a difficult thing.

I miss the level of intimacy which I did have with Hannah. It's difficult for me to have much time on my own with her because when she's here, there are other children here, too, and they do tend to compete for my attention. What still worries me is that when she's with me and another child, she's jealous and this comes out in aggression—she bites the other child and pushes her out of the way—but I know the other child needs me as much as she does.

ALEX. We're very consistent about food. The children eat the same as we do; if they don't want it they don't have to have it, but we don't specially make things to cater to their whims.

JENNY. Everyone seems to get a different favorite at different times among the children, but nobody is everyone's favorite. We talk about that a lot, and the difference between the biological and the nonbiological parents.

When Gill came she had been living with foster parents and she was a dreadful child, either completely passive or in a terrible tantrum.

I enjoy the kids a lot and, besides, I feel it's the right thing to do. I don't want a kid of my own in the nuclear family situation—I don't think I could cope at all, I'd probably batter it!

If I wanted to have a child into this collective, it wouldn't be my decision entirely, it would have to be with everybody's agreement. But I don't feel the need to have a baby with all these around me.

CAROL. I think the weekly crèche meetings are important so we keep closely in touch with each other's child-rearing habits. So when Sam, Hannah, Gill or Misha comes for a night or a weekend here, they get treated very much the same way as they would at home. For example, if the kids have a nap at one o'clock and are put on the potty before they go to bed, I try to stick to the same routine. There were some teething troubles with the children the first few nights they stayed here, but now they've settled down.

ALEX. As the kids get older we'd like to give them more choice about where they'd like to be.

JAN. When you're bringing up children in a way that's so different from anything that's been done before, it's more than a worry—it's a gigantic responsibility. I've come up against so many conflicts in myself about the bringing up of children that I feel very depressed about it—the anxiety of not really knowing if I'm doing the right thing. And even if I'm not, it's been taken out of my hands, because although legally Sam is my responsibility, I couldn't possibly say, "O.K., you lot, I'm fucking off now and I'm taking Sam with me!" I just couldn't, it would be a monstrous thing to do—to them and to Sam—but more particularly to them because Sam is only two and a half.

I definitely feel different about Sam than I do about the other three. That's not to say I don't love the others in my own way, especially Misha because I helped deliver Misha—she was born at home, straight into the collective situation.

If I had another child I wouldn't bring it up in the same way because of the difficulties of ties. I mean, if a marriage breaks up there are problems over custody. Well, in a sense, a marriage has broken up between me and Abbey Road, and although we all get on in varying degrees, the marriage is definitely breaking up. And what happens when one or another of us wants to move to another town or country? What happens? I can't see myself spending the rest of my days in Leeds. For instance, for the last nine or ten months I've been having quite a steady relationship with Diane, who doesn't want to stay in Leeds. She's spent all her life in Leeds—she's a Leeds woman—and now she wants to move on and I'll just have to let her go. If I have to choose between her and Sam, I've got to choose Sam.

It's not just Sam, it's all the other grown-ups involved. But when it comes down to it, it's Sam I feel fucked up about. It's as if I've only got quite recently awakened maternal instincts—I don't think Sam has noticed them because I don't treat him any differently. I think a two-year-old is too young to have a concept of mother. He never calls me Mummy, he calls me Jan; but I wouldn't want a child to call me Mummy anyway.

CAROL. At the conference in Newcastle, I noticed our kids just trotted off, smiling and talking to everyone, while some of the kids were so clinging. One woman cried because she'd missed all the conference because her kids wouldn't leave her be.

SEX AND LOVE

ALEX. I think it is difficult to reconcile the relationships outside the house to the people you're living with in the house. I'm sleeping with two women outside the house, Una and Britt, so I'm close to them sexually; but I'm close to Annie in a day-to-day way, although with her I have no sexual relationship.

Una and I felt we were only seeing each other in really nice settings—late at night and with music. But then, through the crèche meetings and through the kids, we've had to talk out disagreements about shitty diapers, and that seems more real. You can't make a split between your romantic fantasies and day-to-day reality—I've had to realise that.

UNA. I feel I can't have anyone taking me for granted sexually, which seemed to happen in the marriage.

ALEX. I think once you lose the fear that the person is going to disappear out of your life, the jealousy isn't so bad. I think we all get a buzz out of the people that are around us being happy and high, and one of the ways that people get happy is through sexual and love relationships. And I think the way things are structured here is to get the most out of each other's happiness and see that it's not at your expense. Though sometimes I do feel hurt and lost, most of the time I want the people I love to be happy.

ALBERT. I have multiple sexual relationships, two in the house and two out of the house, and it gets very tense and neurotic for me at times. I have big heavy freak-outs because I feel one person is rejecting me, and then I go and try to sort it out. I get jealous of Tony and Lisa because they've been together longer and that makes them closer to each other, as opposed to me.

I've had couple relationships before but it got too monotonous. I want to move around and not get too close to one person. I want a lot of attention but I don't need it all from one person. I feel much happier and freer.

UNA. For me sex with women has been an extension of my friendships. If I have a scene with a man, it starts with sex and you get to know him afterwards. Whereas with a woman, you've known her for months and then you're together one night and it seems perfectly reasonable that you should sleep together. If you have a friendship going beforehand and you sleep together and something goes wrong, because you already have a friendship, then you can sort it out. But if you sleep with a guy and you have no friendship and it doesn't work out, then you don't sleep together again.

It's a problem when you do have a love relationship, how much you give the collective and how much to the couple setup. That's been the main problem in this house. When George and Jenny started their scene I felt Jenny stopped relating to me, but we managed to sort it out and I don't feel so uptight about it any more. I feel this is the reason for lots of freak-outs, that people slip into this couple situation. I don't think it's possible to relate equally to the whole group. Unless the two of you explain that you're removing yourselves from the group for a while, it can become very confusing. Say you have short intensive scenes all the time and you just relate to that person—it's something that takes a long time to sort out because we're so conditioned to living in couples. But if you are going to substitute the collective for the couple, then you can't just take away the bad aspects of the couple, you have to substitute the good ones. For example, the closeness and the support and the feeling that someone cares for you. If you can't get these things you're going to feel very lonely—that warmth and supportive thing has to be catered to.

That's come out in the crèche meetings, too—people felt they weren't getting enough support but instead they were attacking each other and making each other paranoid. And so we all did try to be supportive to each other.

Yes, sexual jealousy does exist here. It's not something I suffer from myself, and I think it happens more between the men than between the women. If I go to a women's group and I'm sleeping with a guy that another woman in the group is also sleeping with, because you see each other so much, you just have to work it through.

For instance, when I first started sleeping with Alex, Britt and I at first felt a bit paranoid towards each other. Then, when we did this play, we got to know each other and worked it through. Communication between the men seems less good.

I can suffer from envy. If I'm sleeping on my own and I can hear two people making love then I might suddenly feel left out. But there is another jealousy which is possessive, and you want to know what that person is doing all the time, you think of them as belonging to you. I don't approve of that.

LISA. Jealousy does arise, though I'm not jealous if someone I'm involved with gets involved with a woman or man I respect, or with a friend of mine. But I got really pissed off when Alex got into a heavy romantic scene. But that's three years ago now.

Jealousy isn't a big thing in this house because we seem to have been working it through for so long.

The thing about couples is, it isn't just about who you're sleeping with, or how many people you're sleeping with—you can be sleeping with six people and still in your head be a couple, or you can just have one sex partner but you don't have to be a couple. I used to think, Oh, God, I can't just sleep with one person, I'll be a couple. But I don't feel that now.

If you're sleeping with a lot of people then that's all you've got time for and you just "do relationships," and I think that's a big drag.

ANNIE. My ideas have also been for sexual openness. It's nothing new to me, the longest monogamous relationship I've had is three months. I used to be very passive and not make decisions for myself. I used to think of myself as promiscuous because I would be sleeping with about three people. But in a way it was nice—I'd be quite high then. But it's different now because I'm more careful and I'm wary about getting into intense scenes where someone becomes dependent on me; that scares me. Now I feel I want honesty and friendship out of my sexual relationships.

Some outsiders seem really upset that me, Lisa and Albert are all living in the same house and me and Lisa were both sleeping with Albert, and yet I haven't found that difficult at all. It's not a great big thing to me, sleeping alone. I quite like it. I went through a stage of being more actively bisexual than I am now—and that was confusing, too. And I've been through periods when I've thought I've just wanted to be lesbian and not sleep with men at all because it was too much of a hassle.

I think it's a slow process, altering your sexual identity. You can't just say yesterday I was heterosexual, today I'm homosexual. I still feel confused about it.

ALEX. I did have a gay relationship, but it didn't really work out and in fact it turned me off the idea of gay relationships. I find it incredibly difficult to trust men sexually—I get feelings like, He just wants me for my body.

TONY. When I was living in a couple situation with Lisa, well, she was the first woman I slept with and I found it difficult to visualize having a relationship with anyone else, though after a while we had an agreement that it would be all right if either of us wanted to go off and sleep with someone else as long as "you stay faithful to me in your head and love me best." We both got into relationships with other people but when my new relationship broke up I turned back to Lisa. But she wasn't around in the way I wanted, which was painful. But I learned to be a more independent person.

JENNY. I'm having a scene with George, who's been here for six months, and I can chart my decline from when he moved in here. I've really gone downhill. I've not gone to see people and not got on with things—I've got to the stage where I almost feel I can't go out on my own. It's a contradictory thing—I want the security of that kind of relationship and at the same time I know intellectually that exclusive relationships are bad for me. I base all my opinions of myself on that one person, and no one can go around reassuring you that you're O.K. all the time—you've got to have other people and other things and to be doing things that you think are important.

TOM. I think there are problems about having sexual and emotional relationships within the collective. They are too public; it brutalizes them, it can diminish the trust and intimacy.

On the other hand, there is a certain freedom of choice—people are different and give different things. There are men and women and a lot of homosexual relating is going on. For all my criticisms, I think it's still better than a lot of nuclear setups, or the emancipated, middle-class position, which is characterized by the marital structure where the husband and wife screw around with lots of dishonesty and argument and bitchiness.

People here lead a very busy, politically active life, which means there isn't always enough time for passionate central relationships, and I can get frustrated by this.

Of course, there are unresolved conflicts here, and I think a problem is that some people would think it ideologically wrong to want to spend a lot of time with one person. It's like colonizing and possessing someone. People don't do it, which I feel is a case of being crucified by one's own values if you are actually happier or closer to one person.

It's badly thought of to show physical jealousy—it does happen, but it's badly thought of.

LISA. I believe that if everyone was left to their own devices people would be open to both sexes. But it's difficult to put into practice, and sleeping with someone of the same sex just because you think you ought to is ridiculous. I used to sleep with women but one way and another, all the relationships ended in complete disaster.

It hurt me a lot more than relationships with men did—perhaps I make myself less vulnerable to men. I expected things to be much better with women—I expected perfect communication, because a lot of the propaganda you read pro lesbianism says, "Oh, it's so marvelous with a woman and this is the ultimate thing." I didn't find that and there's no reason why I should; but I felt let down by that and I wasn't used to being let down by women and I feel very wary about getting into that again. Also there were some women who seemed to be into sleeping with women and having a primary relationship with a man. They didn't sleep with other men because that would threaten the relationship.

I can't ever imagine sharing a room again—I want to be able to sleep alone when I choose.

ALBERT. This is the first time I've learned to treat women as people.

JENNY. It is a bit incestuous at the moment. Almost all the sexual relationships are within the collective. That can put outsiders off and make them feel excluded. And sometimes I feel all the things I can ever talk about are the kids and the other people in the collective.

TONY. We sometimes have discussions in the house about if it's O.K. to have a more private romantic relationship from time to time. I say it is and am identified in the house as someone who is into that. I find it a good way to get to know someone really well. But I'm not for it in a permanent way; I'd get bored with it as a full-time lifestyle.

I suppose now I have multiple relationships. There are three women who I am close to, who I don't necessarily see much of, except for Lisa—we still sleep together occasionally. It goes in phases; sometimes I think I'm settling down into an easy pattern and then someone else comes along and the whole thing is thrown back into the melting pot. I don't know how long that pattern will carry on; perhaps when one gets into one's sixties it becomes physically difficult or perhaps the desire to settle down becomes stronger?

There was a phase when I was trying to encourage myself to get into relationships with men, which I was pushing too hard. I thought of it as an ideal, but nowadays I feel more easy about it. I haven't slept with a man for quite a while—well, six months. I've become more conservative about my sexuality!

JAN. I get on with Lisa a lot better now I've left Abbey Road. One of the reasons our relationship got into difficulty may have been that we slept together for a while, and after that she got hung up and freaked out about the idea of sleeping with women. She just didn't enjoy it—she just thought she should. It's one of the hazards of trying to expand your sexuality, and I'm much more into doing what comes naturally than trying to contrive situations. There are some women involved in the women's movement who feel obligated to get into bisexuality.

POLITICS

GEORGE. What is interesting about this scene is the political consciousness, that people are thinking about what they're doing and questioning their lives. But what is revolutionary about it is that it's being done on a shoestring budget, that the people involved are poor and it's not done on vast incomes. So, economically speaking, if it can be done under these circumstances, it can be done by anybody, and I really think that's important because so much of what has been done in the way of progressive education has been done by people who were really well-off and pooled a lot of their assets into it.

Of course, there are tremendous dissatisfactions with all our ways of life, but the impulse that we have drummed into us is to seek individual solutions. If someone is having a hassle bringing up children, they will look for some way of bringing up *their* children with more help—once again they're looking for an individual solution.

ALEX. We feel that because of the breakdown of the community in the outside world, a lot of misery and mental illness is caused, and that in collective living a lot of these hurdles are got over— by interaction with each other and also by having people around who are often deprived in various ways.

ALBERT. I like being here because people are actually doing things rather than so many political groups where they just talk about them.

SYLVIA. It is very rarely that one happens to come across a woman like Lisa, who really tries to find out exactly what she believes and actually practices it.

LISA. We don't believe that just because somebody's got a degree they should necessarily be able to earn more, so we all decided to share our money. It does get difficult if I feel somebody is lying around all day and I'm sweating away doing modeling at the art school. Then I feel resentful. I wouldn't be prepared to go out to work and share my income with a whole lot of people who did absolutely nothing all day long.

TONY. I wouldn't force myself into a lifestyle just out of political convictions, but I do see how we live as politically important. I see the way you relate to other people as an important political thing, but it's only revolutionary as far as other people can relate to it, particularly the people who live around. We don't want to force our way of living down other people's throats.

We have had a lot of criticism for things like taking the privacy out of our personal lives—with women's groups and men's groups —or for the way we bring up our kids.

JAN. One thing we are united on in this collective is women's liberation. That doesn't mean we believe in grinding underfoot all males. At the first national lesbian conference I had a bad time. There was a small minority of women who really believed in exterminating males, and I said, "But listen, I've got a male child." And one woman said, "Well, I've got a male child, too, and I've sent him to live with his father and I never want to see him again." There were only about three or four women like that but it really freaked me out. It pissed me off, too, because I think it gives lesbianism a bad name.

ALEX. I want our idea about collective living and the crèche to spread. If you're just an isolated unit is doesn't change anything or mean much. Already, since we began, two other similar collectives have been set up in Leeds. Our left-wing friends who are well-off and well-educated seem more wary of what we're doing than our working-class neighbors. But perhaps it's not so surprising, because working-class families see the practical side of sharing and middle-class people get caught up in psychiatric angst-type dimensions of the way we live.

We meet a lot of working-class mothers in the community play group and talk to them about how we live. A lot of them are very positive about it and see how free and happy our kids are.

A few of us in the crèche are getting more involved in the broader campaigns going on, both in Leeds and nationally, for more community-controlled child-care facilities for the under-fives. Right now we're fighting to get money from the authorities for the community play group our kids go to. Only by getting decent wages for play group work can local working-class parents get fully involved and committed.

LISA. I see it as a fairly political thing, the way I'm living, something that I hope will spread much more widely. I don't see it as just relieving the burden from the mother, but also the bringing up of kids to relate to more than just one person, so they don't reproduce the extreme dependency on the mother when they grow up. They won't fixate on one person and see that person as being all wrapped up in their identity.

UNA. The women's movement has influenced the way I relate to other women. I used to be very competitive and I think I only wanted to know men. As soon as there was a man around, I felt I had to compete with any other woman for his attention. I used to be very insecure and touchy. All this has changed.

If someone criticized me, I couldn't cope. I used to try to change myself all the time to suit the guy I was with. I became his woman, the image that he wanted. But through the women's movement I realized I couldn't go on doing that and I tried to find out Who am I? What do I want? And to accept myself as I really am. I feel far more confident now.

ANNIE. I think the women's movement has done a lot for me, though sometimes I feel I'm as weedy and pathetic as I was before. It's definitely increased my consciousness. My awareness is sharper—I wouldn't get into many of the situations I used to get into. Also, I'm less frightened. I'm not too frightened to teach now.

LISA. Everyone in this house is pretty politically focused. It took us about a year to get to know people in Leeds. It was very dreary in the beginning; we were just setting up the collective. Now I'm very busy with meetings et cetera and I'm much happier.

SYLVIA.   From my point of view, people try to attend too many political meetings. Although these are essential and extremely valuable, it can lead to people not being able to sort out their personal problems first, to adequately cope with the necessary but boring routine of everyday life.

WHERE TO?

ALEX.   I see my future tangled up with the kids for a long time. I wouldn't want to go off for long periods till the kids were five or six. Then, as long as it was worked out so plenty of the others were here, I might travel for a year or two.

   I don't think all of us are going to spend the rest of our lives in Leeds but that the kids should be based here and we can move around, and that there will be continual interaction between all of us.

LISA.   It is a commitment to the future. Sometimes all of us feel rather tied down because we think we're stuck living in Leeds— we can't suddenly go off to Africa, which if it's just one parent or two parents, they can. But we're much freer in terms of being able just to get up and go off for three months or longer if we want to.

ANNIE.   I feel committed to Leeds till the kids are five or six and after that I'm not sure. At the moment I still think I'm suffering from the shock at the responsibility of having children. Three years ago I'd never had anything to do with children. Normally, if someone had four kids, they'd have taken at least four years to have them. Nobody else seems to feel this, but I still feel I've been hit on the head with a hammer and I just can't believe that deep down, it's happening.

TONY. I feel committed to the collective for the next few years. I'm coming to a stage where I want to put down roots in a city, though I haven't quite worked out the terms.

I'd like to be free to be able to go off to America. It should theoretically be possible for anyone to go off for a year, if it's carefully worked out.

JENNY. I don't think much about the future because there's no pattern to my life. I can't look forward to the normal events that people structure their lives around. I can't look forward ten years and see myself with the same people, as a normal married couple might expect.

My parents have been here and seen the kids and I think they've accepted that they're not going to get any grandchildren from me. At first I avoided telling them how I was living. Then my sister and I had a long talk about it, and we decided we'd either got to start talking to them on a human level now or we'd got to go on not communicating until they die or we die, and it seemed so silly. So at Christmas we both went home and had a good long talk with them about the women's movement and everything else we were doing, and now it's much better.

LISA. I feel a basic security. If, for instance, something happened and I was forced to go and live in Newcastle, then I'd join the women's group and make new friends. I was brought up in the army, so I've always moved around. It doesn't scare me—you move to a new place and you slowly get to know people.

TOM. Is it all really worth it? Perhaps I'd rather live on my own. Then my connection would be more to the kids and less to the other adults.

GEORGE. There could be such a thing as a collective staying together for the sake of the children, just as sometimes you get a marriage staying together for the sake of the children.

The supportive relationships between the adults tend to shift and change. What is more worrying is major estrangements, should they come. This seems to me to be the rock-bottom problem of this collective: the biological parents have power over the kids that the nonparents just don't have, although the nonparents are giving just as much in the way of care. All they can do is to make one gigantic act of resignation. This is all very fine as long as the relationships are going well, but if some kind of estrangement takes place then this becomes a sharp conflict.

The nonbiological parents suffer from insecurity, the acute insecurity of having no legal power over *their* children.

A time of crisis for the collective.

What I feel is that this collective might break down in three or four or five years' time. Too many people may want to go their separate ways. Just now, Jan is sick of Leeds and she is thinking of moving on. Everyone is worried: what happens to Sam? But finally this doesn't matter—what does is that people have got together for a bit to learn from one another and to support each other through that extremely difficult period of raising young children. The women, through close contact, have discovered each other as women, as people. For the men all the mystique of diapers and housework and child-care has gone. The way our society traps and isolates young parents doesn't work, and leads anyway to the breakdown of marriages and to boring and frustrating lives.

Something else I was impressed by was that people were allowed, in their words, to "freak out," or, in the words of the straight society, "get extremely depressed, tearful and angry." These periods were at the least tolerated and at best confronted with warmth and interest. Nobody was frightened of the struggle to live and the struggle to survive.

There is a great deal of music, laughter and fun in communal living. Everyone knows each other pretty well, almost everyone has slept together. So things like sharing the bathroom, being naked around the place and having rows seem natural and unconstrained. People know about each other and have also learned to express their emotions fully.

Would I have brought up my children this way had I known about Leeds when they were young?

Certain things I'd have found difficult: my relationship with my children is private and possessive, and I might well have been jealous of their not having a prime attachment to me. Also the giving of love and energy to small children who aren't mine— I'm not very interested in other people's babies, but perhaps that's just because the relationship is never intimate enough. Maybe I'd have grown out of the difficulties if I'd tried, and I can see the advantages are so enormous.

Directly I had my first child I felt bound to provide such amenities as a garden, toys, the right nursery school, friends. I felt that if I didn't provide the very best of all these things my child would be handicapped for life. So I struggled to make a safe, bright, clean, middle-class world which was really quite alien to me and for that matter, alien to the father of my children.

If I'd been part of something like Leeds I'd have seen that many of these things are easy to come by if shared—and that the others aren't really necessary. I'd have been part of a peer group of intelligent, changing, sharing people—I wouldn't have been lonely and frozen in my own tight nuclear world. How different would my children have been? There is no way of telling. **"**

SIX MONTHS LATER

The Leeds commune replies.

First, to put the "Time Of Crisis" that you wrote about into perspective a bit, here's a rundown on some of the changes since then.

Carol and her two boys, Sean and Brian, have moved to the States. Carol's got a job in a women's health center in Los Angeles; Sean and Brian are at a free school there. Una and Jenny have left Penny Lane and moved into a larger house in the same street as Jan's house. They've moved in together with Mark, Annie's cousin, who's moved here from Nottingham, and

Kate—a woman with a five-year-old boy. Tom's chosen (temporarily) to live on his own in Penny Lane. Sylvia's husband came out of prison and he's sharing one of the crèche days—he and Sylvia have just got a flat nearby.

Faced with several people getting involved within a short space of time, we resolved that since we were afraid of spreading the kids too thinly, no new adults should take any of the crèche day turns unless we simply couldn't manage to fill one from our existing numbers. We want to preserve continuity too.

We had an all-day marathon "annual crèche meeting" to celebrate our first anniversary and to assess our failures and achievements. There was a really good and hopeful atmosphere. The "Time of Crisis" over control of Sam seemed a long way in the past (that's not to say we've solved it forever). We dwelt a lot on how, if we were collective with the kids, we needed to have a more collective responsibility for each other's financial and job situations, so that it wasn't so arbitrary who was working and who was free to do child-care. We ended up setting up a fund creating limited wages for child-care.

Talking about our working lives—Annie's started working full time at the play group you mention; Una's working full time as a civil servant; Albert's likely to have to work full time soon and Tom will teach full time, more or less. Otherwise our main work pattern is part-time or temporary jobs; for example, Lisa's getting a small wage from the National Women's Information Service set up in Leeds recently (WIRES) ; Jenny has just started another few weeks of clerical work (around Christmas, she's off to Australia for a holiday paid for by our international crèche connection, George, who went back to his university job in Sydney some months ago).

An odd twist on the way we see parenthood as not necessarily tied to mothering or fathering—Alex's friend, Britt, is pregnant by him but they've worked out that he won't be as closely involved with bringing up the child as the people Britt lives with. Another collectively reared child on the way.

So you see, our setup is not static.

Second, we passed round what you wrote, Nell, and came up with the following. All of us felt you concentrated too much on "us adults" and barely gave any idea of what you thought the kids were like and what sort of people they are.

Somehow we felt you gave too little emphasis to the values behind our living collectively and bringing up our kids the way we do. We believe it's possible, practical and important to start trying to work out alternatives to the family in the here and now. Previously, most people who supported socialism have left their own lives and their own children out of their socialism. That's probably been a big factor in why socialism has, so often, turned sour.

Nell, you highlight things like our stress on the need for consistency, the form of our child-care, without bringing out what we try to be consistent about—the content of it all. We would have said more about how we've been encouraging the kids to share, care for each other, be self-reliant, learn group awareness, develop freer sex roles outside the usual boys-active, girls-passive routine. And how we've been discouraging competitiveness, favoritism, pecking orders and rigid sex roles.

We'd also have tried to explain why we've chosen to live in a multiracial, working-class, inner-city area when we could have lived elsewhere. None of us agree with trying to give our kids a privileged life or bringing them up in well-off middle-class stress, which strangely enough usually turns out children who grow up experiencing the struggles of ordinary people for a better life as some sort of threat to them. Although we do see ourselves as a collective, this doesn't mean we see ourselves as part of a communes movement. We're trying to work out new forms of living and child-care relationships, because we don't think much of the usual ones, that's all.

How you saw our various relationships set us buzzing. Several of us thought you made us sound like a sexual free-for-all, and very incestuous at that. So we do want to say that, in reality, most of the time we all have outside interests, activities and relationships unconnected with the crèche and people in it. These can sometimes be more important than those to do with the crèche. We are much more collective over the kids than among ourselves —some of us don't see each other between crèche meetings (now once a fortnight).

And on sex, sure our relationships and their patterns are unusual, but without going into who hasn't slept with whom, it's stretching it to say nearly all of us have slept with everyone else, even excluding the men with each other. Maybe the best way to put it into perspective is that, on average, most of us spend half or more of our nights sleeping alone. Compare that to the usual shared marriage bed. Time alone, celibacy, monogamous relationships—these can and do exist within our setup too, even if not in the same way as usual.

I think a lot of people get shunted onto tramlines and they go along having to make decisions not based on where they're at as people, as individuals, but based on the needs of their domestic situation.

5. NO TIES: MARY

Mary pinpoints the problems of the independent existence. If you decide the nuclear family isn't for you, what else is there? If you decide you want to have babies in the "right" situation, and the right situation never quite happens, what do you do?

I find Mary's piece particularly fascinating because it is one of my fantasies, perhaps one of everyone's fantasies—to create a situation where you have "no ties" and therefore can enter into life very wildly, experiencing each thing for itself, not as a rung on a preconceived ladder.

Mary is twenty-eight. She lives in a house with six other people, each with his own room and shared kitchen and sitting room; they have been living there for two years, eating together in the evenings and being some kind of family for each other. Now it's suddenly breaking up. Paul is going to live with Annie, Mo is going to live with Alex, Sue is going to live with Chris. Everyone is pairing off into couples and, feeling that the communal situation impairs their relationships, they're going to move out. **99**

WHERE FROM?

MARY.   I did Social Science at Liverpool University. My generation felt they had achieved independence. I wondered whether we were going to follow it through and make something of it or whether everyone was ultimately going to fall into the nuclear family thing, having simply put it off, like we put off any kind of responsibility, including children. We were on the pill.

NOW

If you don't have fulfillment of a relationship, you're much more likely to get up off your backside and do things. I feel that simply because I don't have to consult anybody about what I do. I have done a lot of things that otherwise I simply wouldn't have done, like gone and worked in a therapeutic community or traveled. It's something to do with being free to throw yourself into a situation in a total way, being able to abandon yourself to a particular experience, like when Carol and I go off somewhere and London ceases to exist.

I do find that when I go somewhere I can get totally involved in my surroundings, operating in a free-floating, visitor-from-outer-space way. I can get a fascinating picture of everyone's life and yet no one can pin me down—I'm traveling through. Yet I don't have to be preoccupied with anything or anyone I've left behind, like oh, poor Mom's looking after the kids, or my husband might be going off with someone else.

Also, I've had the freedom to spend my money on intangible things like going to America. I've done lots of different things and taken long holidays, so I don't expect material security. I try to work in jobs that seem meaningful to me and then, when I've developed and left the job behind, I try to move onto something new. Work is important to me insofar as it makes demands on me, stretches me.

I think a lot of people get shunted onto tramlines and they go along having to make decisions not based on where they're at as people, as individuals, but based on the needs of their domestic situation. And because I'm not responsible for anyone, any choice that I make is geared solely to my own feelings about it. In some ways that's great, because it gives you a lot of freedom, but freedom is a very frightening thing.

Now everyone's leaving here I can't but feel the carpet slipping under my feet. It's a big shake-up and it's happened so suddenly —one minute everyone is generating a family feeling round the supper table, and the next minute everyone can desert you. The most important thing in their lives is the other half of the couple. So I feel in some ways as if I'm floating—they weren't couples when we started living together and now they are.

CHILDREN

I played around with my freedom as an independent individual who left home in order to live on my own. I just had myself to please and I could be totally myself. Contraception has become like refrigerators—everyone has contraception. Because you're given the choice, nobody makes a decision.

I am at an age when I start to wonder about making choices like having children. Physiologically I will be getting old to have my first child soon—your bone structure starts to harden or something. Men can fantasize about having children when they're older, but for me time is running out. If I want to set up some kind of situation where I can have kids, I must do something about it.

Ultimately, you have children because you want to have someone's children. Now there's a strong part of me that wants to have children. What do I do if I don't happen to find the other part of the bargain—the man? Do I compromise and think about having someone's child who I don't see myself caring strongly about or staying with?

SEX AND SEX

For some time I lived with Steve on a boat thirty-three feet by six feet. Emotionally it was a very secure experience. It was "us" against "them" and the relationship worked really well because we lived in our own little world; we were the only permanent thing in one another's lives, apart from the inside of the boat. But coming back to London, our whole world expanded. I found myself in a living situation that brought out different sides of me.

I often wonder how much I was suppressing myself, because we did lots of things to the boat but we did it in a very mutual, shared way. When I got a room of my own I found out what I wanted to do, and whole areas of conflict sprang up between us.

On the boat we lived from hand to mouth. Steve did potato picking and when we were hungry, we picked cabbages from people's gardens and got dog bones from the butchers. It became a very unreal experience and I wanted to come back to London. I really do like things like glasses of wine. My standard of living can fluctuate quite a bit—particularly when I'm away from the temptations of the consumer society—but in the end, I begin to feel starved of things I've been used to, like pretty clothes. Although I look back on that time when with great nostalgia, it was very much a close couple situation.

I think coupledom is a bit like a contagious disease—when you come into contact with it, you can't help but be affected by it. I think I'd be a lot more adequate as an individual on my own if I wasn't surrounded by couples.

When Paul or Annie's friends ring up they say, "Is Paul or Annie in?" and I feel like saying, "No, Paul-or-Annie is out." It's as if they are no longer individuals but one conglomerate mass.

I found, when I came back to London with Steve, in social situations I was identified with him, and perhaps because we were very different, I found that very destructive.

If you don't get married very young and you develop as an individual, it's more difficult to allow yourself to get molded by a relationship. It strikes me that because the relationships we have are more insecure than ever before, they are also more demanding.

It's amazing how much energy I dissipated on my emotional life at university. It was all a kind of endless wheeling and dealing. I could have been getting on with other things. Does it point to the fact that everyone is looking for the ultimate security of the couple?

Then there's the economic security—couples buying a house —immediately their financial situation gets involved; how much more difficult it then is for one of them to go to the other end of the world.

Last summer I went through a period of sleeping with half a dozen different people. That was quite interesting because it was the closest I've come to sleeping around. And I enjoyed it in a way because when I'm in a physical relationship, I feel good, desirable and all those kinds of things. And I was getting that without the emotional hang-ups, so I had a lot of freedom because I didn't feel something was desperately lacking in my life. But it all fizzled out, probably because the relationships were purely physical. Since that time I haven't slept with anybody, and I do feel I've become asexual.

It doesn't work very well for me sexually—not being in settled relationships. I realized, when I split up with my first boyfriend after two years, what I'd lost, because we had always had a good relationship physically and it was always there, "on tap," as you might say. Since that time it's a problem—I find it difficult to combine physical and mental relationships.

The other night I got in a situation with a man I know. He put his arms round me and I froze; I felt it was like an exposure. I'd kept myself to myself for so long I couldn't—so I escaped. I feel sexually closed up; I don't feel desirable because there's no one around telling me I am. Yet I feel glad that I know I can be on my own and that I'll never fall into the trap of clinging to someone because I'm terrified of being alone. One friend of mine started sleeping with a guy because she wanted someone to keep her warm for the winter.

When you live with six other people it's possible to avoid one of them if you aren't getting on. You can avoid confrontation only too easily and you avoid the opportunity to develop a relationship with that person—it's shunted into a dead-end siding—and you therefore avoid your own emotional growth.

POLITICS

You know the saying that marriage is the last resort of the un-
imaginative—a lot of people marry to give them a structure
within which to act. So if something is going wrong in their
lives, they don't have to blame themselves, they can blame their
situation—"I had to consider my wife and kids."

Women's liberation should really help men a lot. If a man is
married to someone about whom he can say, "I don't have to fend
for this woman," he can at last make choices of his own—to do
what he wants to do—and his woman need no longer live in a
cocoon.

*Often I feel so weighed down by responsibilities. This morning
I took my son Jem to school and when we got there we discovered
we (or he?) had forgotten his swimming things, his recorder
book, his weaving stick, his knitting wool. A little girl helped
us search in the remains of a bonfire and we found a half-burnt
cleft stick which we all agreed would do for a weaving stick with
a little paring down and scrubbing. She had a beautiful one her
father had made out of the Christmas tree, and I immediately
felt guilty.*

*What had I been doing all weekend that I hadn't helped Jem
practise his recorder or find a forked stick? I had put his swim-
mings things all ready by the front door but we had both managed
not to see them.*

*Fleetingly, I longed for a proper middle-class, respectable family
life—a husband who made weaving sticks out of Christmas trees. I
thought of Mary and her ambiguous desire for responsibility. I
thought of my overwhelming desire to be totally without responsibility. How can I find a balance?*

We're a tree. The household's the trunk. Different people,
different needs, a solid body which (amazingly) grows.
Smoothly, with tangles, laughter, anguish, we grow. The roots
are the children. The sap is the love between us all.

6. ANARCHY: BRIGHTON

Brighton was the most anarchic setup I went to. Nobody was
trying to be good, nobody was trying to find a political solution
to life, nobody was "trying" to be anything much—they were
just living together.

When I first arrived I found it alarming. David attacked me
for being rich and I tried to pretend I wasn't. Mike attacked me
for nosing into other people's lives. Sue just remained herself
(she is a completely uncontrolling person).

By the end of the first weekend, however, I was quite high.
Everybody was, all the time, expressing what they thought about
each other. The children were remarkably free. Finally—after

only two days, but it felt like a lifetime—David drove me to the station in his diesel van, with Jem beside me. We both fell asleep on the train back to London. I came away believing that most people don't have enough drama in their lives—they are too frightened. Drama is exhilarating.

The Brighton house is large, late Victorian, overlooking a green space and a few minutes from the beach. A tame white rabbit runs about the house, chewing the coconut matting and pissing on the beds of people he doesn't like. In the backyard there is the homemade pottery works and the kiln.

These are the people who live there:

Sue, thirty-five, who was married to (but is now divorced from) Peter. Their children spend every weekend with him, sometimes at Brighton, sometimes in London. The children are Lucinda, ten; Clara, eight; and Ben, seven.

Zapp, twenty-one, a young painter.

David, thirty-one, whose children—Tim, six; and Adam, five—stay weekends. Married to Emma, who lives elsewhere in Brighton. David makes oak furniture.

Simon, thirty-five, who among other things is a writer. His children—Jenny, six; and Jake, seven—spend most weekends and sometimes stay longer. Married to Carol, who also lives in the same town.

Mike, twenty-five, who lives in the basement which is self-contained. Mike and Sue are lovers.

Martin, twenty-five, who designs solar water-heating systems. A focus of discontent, perhaps, like the white rabbit; "a scapegoat," said Simon.

They met in various ways—through a Sufi meditation center, at the Trentishoe Fair (a celebration of the earth—as Sue said, "It was a marvelous week, confirming the solidarity of people who had dropped out").

The house belongs to Peter who, since Sue and he split up, lives in London. The other adults pay rent and share the space.

Since I was last there, Sue has given up her big bare room to the children and she slept on a mattress in a small back room.

She said she didn't mind really where she slept. When Mike, in a rage, burnt her wig, she said she didn't mind that either, it wasn't particularly special. "Mike felt like doing it," she said.

Nearly all of Sue's life takes place in this house or on the beach or up in the garden. Her children are excluded from very little.

On Sunday, we took a bottle of wine and went up to their garden. Sitting up on the hill overlooking the sea . . . drinking . . . talking. The garden was laid out by a Greek and has been left the same—with box hedges, and a little hut with a mirror hanging in it and a tiny cupboard and pinups and Greek family photographs. Oddly enough, the hillside overlooking the sea is quite like Greece.

Sue plants everything in circles—the radishes, the beans, spinach and lettuces. "I like circles," she says.

She tells us how she once went off for a week with a friend, sleeping in ditches, and one morning he didn't want her to be there anymore so she set off across the fields carrying her bag, in the drizzle, and she didn't see him for six months.

The children water the vegetables and talk to some people passing on ponies. Lucinda, who keeps a family of guinea pigs and wants to live on a farm, tells of how she wants a pony of her own and never to wear a dress.

Sue and the children walked out the other day—Sue was sick of being a landlady. She stayed away for a fortnight and when she came back everyone was building a new kitchen.

She hates waste and dresses herself stylishly in clothes from rummage sales.

I couldn't decide if I should include Mike's rather angry speech about the house and ownership. But I thought I wanted to because, again and again, this is such a problem—capital, the landlady, responsibility, equality. This is so much at the center of the problem of why so many communes fail to get off the ground, or flounder, and why people remain in the nuclear family situation, or repeat it again when it has failed them once.

So here it is as a part of this informative section. **99**

MIKE. Obviously, for me, the house to a large extent exists in flux, according to Sue's relating to me or not. She is definitely the sole possessor by virtue of her marriage. This household exists because of her wishes, respected—although finally limited—by the owner, her ex-husband, Peter. If, for instance, Sue moved out, I think the household would fold. Peter would probably repossess the house to live in it himself. Primarily this house exists as a home for Clara, Ben, Lucinda and their mother. This means that everyone else is to a degree dependent upon Sue for the present roof over our heads.

One of the dreams that we have is for all of us to move into a big house in the country where we have an equality of ownership. Basically I regard this house as temporary.

WHERE FROM?

SIMON. I'm the son of a writer. I split with my wife, Carol, about a year ago. I don't think we were ever happy in the couple situation; for some time before we split up we were sharing houses.

I'm so over-trained that the Welfare can't find me a job. I'm a bird brain surgeon; I trained at Sussex University.

ZAPP. I left home because there were lots of things I wanted to experience directly. I wanted to spread my wings and "go forth."

MARTIN. I'd been dropping by here to crash occasionally for six months before I took a room.

I was squatting in a house in London which was a hellhole full of junkies. Also, I spent some time in a commune in the south of France where they were growing their own food. They spent all day working in the fields and seemed to have no time for anything but eating—all the time was spent frantically cultivating food. I feel there is more to life than eating and shitting.

DAVID. It was pure chance I came to be here. I left Emma, my wife, and had to go somewhere, so it was here. But I don't feel it's a satisfying alternative for me, as it stands.

My marriage went wrong with children. Having the children ruined everything, though paradoxically we're both extremely attached to them. But it destroyed everything and I really envy people without children—the freedom they have. I don't believe some of the people in this house understand what it is to have your freedom curtailed in a very serious way.

I don't see how to solve the problem. Many people feel the commune will help to create a larger unit and share the children, but I don't know that this works for me.

Emma wasn't a natural mother. Though she is a good mother, being tied up in the house doesn't bring out the best of her. The strain of looking after two children so close together (they're six and seven now) really distorts one's personality deep down; it's not the kind of thing that makes one lovable.

I have been very happy with the children and with Emma, but a large part of the time it was hellish. As much from economic reasons as from anything else—just trying to make ends meet.

Also, society is intolerant of children—enough isn't done to make life rich for them. Not so much economically but in terms of tolerance, for example, getting somewhere to live. Society's demands are heavier and heavier—you have to be a superman as an earner, and then you have no time to yourself.

There is an ethic in this house of not wanting much money so sometimes I start feeling guilty about it. But I have been really poor, and I suspect most of the people here have come from comfortable backgrounds and don't quite understand what it's like to have children and no money.

SUE. We had the format of a conventional life when I was married to Peter. I was completely committed to the marriage, Peter's work and the children.

We ran a community center for five years and lived there. Peter was responsible for everything, and I ran a women's group for women who had dropped out of everything and were totally unable to relate to the system or control their own lives. I was involved in everything Peter did—it was a very strong relationship —we worked side by side, as it were.

I think my relationship with him was as to a solid father who knew where he was going, also as an ideal father to the children. Exploring each other's emotional depth wasn't part of it. More husband, less lover, if you like. By nature I'm very monogamous; as long as the marriage was working there was never any question of anyone else. Apart from that, with three small children, there wasn't much energy left.

From the time my last child was born I sensed that my marriage was changing, that there might come a time when it was right to leave.

Then we went abroad in an official job. I organized a child welfare center, which was a creative outlet for me, but gradually I questioned all the work I'd been doing and whether outside people could ever help. I got to a state of mind of believing that the only thing you could ever do for other people was to be yourself with as much integrity as possible—be who you really are so other people can take energy from you.

So I was questioning the whole value of what Peter and I had ever done and removing myself from it. For the last six months abroad I did no work at all. I just used to walk about and sit on the beach and read and try to *begin* to find out who I really was, because until then, up to the age of thirty, I'd been living on other people's standards. And that process has gone on.

By that time I realized the marriage really had finished and I had an affair. This quite blew my mind as it was the first scene I'd had with anybody else. It was totally sexual, so I got very high on sex for the first time, and it moved me into a different way of looking at the world, which I realized I had to get into, the whole of fantasy and imagination and sensuality which I'd cut out of my life—it opened doors and made me see I could get into that world.

The affair itself came to an end (as we got separated geographically when we came back to England) but the things it had done to my head went on.

Our marriage was clearly in a very rocky position, and we sat in this house in Brighton all winter wondering what the hell to do. I wasn't so open then—I didn't want to hurt him. He was so shattered and I was shattered, too—I was taking steps to, perhaps, shatter the children's lives.

I'd never been a completely traditional wife. I never gave posh dinner parties or kept the house spick-and-span with furniture polish. I've never actually made a physical "home." All the time with Peter I needed to be valued for my intellectuality and not other things—I thought it was degrading to be valued as a woman. It may have been the whole grammar school part of my education.

After we finally decided to split I took the children to Spain for three months to try and think what we should do. I felt that Peter didn't want the marriage to end, didn't want to do this to the children; I felt that the responsibility was totally mine.

We came back to Brighton. Peter moved out and lodgers moved in, and from that point on I withdrew from everybody and everything. I moved into one room; the children slept next door and I gave them the minimum physical and emotional attention that I could. I didn't even wash dishes and I hardly ever cleaned anything. I fed the children once a day, but not very well. I rejected everything and went into a shell. If the children said, "Oh, Mom, I'm not getting out of bed," I couldn't get into any hassle with them or say, "Oh, yes you are, you've got to get out of bed and go to school." So, lots of the time they didn't go to school. Nothing much got done and the lodgers in the house (who were a pretty straight lot—I didn't have any contact with them either) frequently grumbled about the mess.

I had no money problems. I had a roof over my head and Peter was supporting us, so I let go on that level, but I was very tight about any emotional contact with anyone. I spent all day in my room painting. And then I had ridiculous affairs with people— purely sexual—saying to myself Well, I'm a free woman, but, of course, it never worked.

I seemed to splatter my broken self on the house and all that I came in touch with. Then, slowly, slowly, from the mess that I was, helped by the warm love of a different bunch of people in and around the house, I felt that I could slowly, slowly, move and grow again.

NOW

SIMON. In the autumn, everyone cooked separately—in a tiny kitchen there were seven different people cooking. I felt that this was Sue's wish, that she discouraged cooking together, that she needed her isolation. Gradually several of us opted to cook together. But nobody liked the idea of a "kitty"; they wanted to pay for the food in a haphazard fashion, which made problems. Now we put about three pounds a week each in the kitty, and, so far, it's working well.

DAVID. I have considered what it would be like living in a ordinary boarding house and I know it would be pretty awful. At the same time it has a morbid fascination for me. In a way it's too easy here and nice, and really I should suffer a bit more. Perhaps I don't appreciate this house as much as I should. In a way it is security, and Sue is an extraordinarily nice person, but I feel it doesn't satisfy me emotionally. I don't find a great sense of community here. This could be my peculiar nature but it's also, partly, that I am older than the rest and feel, if for no other reason, a lack of understanding.

SIMON. When I first visited the house I was courting Sue, and then much later, when I moved in, that left a residual tension. In a way we keep our distance—we meet in the kitchen and sitting room but we don't visit one another's rooms much.

Since I've worked with David, building the new kitchen, I've begun to feel an affection for him. That's after living together in this house for eight months. Some things happen very slowly here.

Up till now—the new kitchen—Sue has consulted with us, but the decisions have been hers.

SUE. When the basement became vacant it seemed right that Mike should move in. We, both wanted to try living in the same house. Various other people wanted the basement. I spent an evening with David and Simon who both wished the house to develop in different directions. I explained where I was at with Mike and why it was important to me that he should move in. They were both very generous and said O.K., my needs could take preference to their wishes. That was so nice and I felt warmed and cared for emotionally. Mike and I couldn't have taken this step against their wishes.

MIKE. I don't think I would have moved in if Sue and her children had been living alone. I think that would have enclosed the situation beyond all of our abilities to cope with its problems. As it is, if Sue and I break up, the effect on Ben, Clara and Lucinda would be minimal.

MARTIN. I feel here everything is constantly in question. It would be impossible for any power maniac to get a foothold here.

SUE. Ever since I came to live in this house I feel I've been attempting to live on an intuitive level and I've been cutting out my brain. I could see that up until that time I'd been living through my brain, and it got me nowhere. I began to do all sorts of things, like painting, that were coming from my guts, and the minute I began to *think* about it, I was thinking in the conventional way that just blocked out any deeper intuitions. I couldn't even read a book or have a cerebral conversation with anybody.

About this house, I've been living in this way, and if something feels right, the right thing to do at the right time from an intuitive sense, I let it happen. And if it feels wrong, I try to stop it.

MIKE. The big hassle with Sue is that there are so many different roles—the landlady-tenant, husband-wife, outside-inside. It's just unbearable at times. I feel consumed with doubt. There's no simple way, you can't just jump into it, it's the creating of a way of life.

MARTIN. I don't consider this my home because, for the last few weeks I've been under fire for not paying rent.

SUE. Everyone in this house has problems about work. We're trying to get this pottery together because we want to earn money with some artistic expression of us as a unit, and to get it together in our way and not in someone else's way.

Simon is writing a book, Zapp paints lovely pictures, Mike wants to make films. But these aren't money-making, so people have a problem about having enough to subsist on. The pottery was all sorts of things. Mike wanted to develop something together—something we could all do—and a feeling that work should be part of everyday life and a reflection of everyday life. Something that got the house together in some constructive project rather than just sitting around talking . . so many different strands.

ZAPP. It would be very good to be self-sufficient, if the pottery could sustain our needs. Since we began there has been great pleasure in working together.

MARTIN. For a long time I was making money washing up part time in a restaurant, enough to pay my rent. But when I gave that up I found I could concentrate more on pursuing my idea to do with solar energy stations. At the same time I came under fire for being improvident, which made another difficulty. I can't go on the Social Security—I find it takes away my self-esteem just too much—so I get by doing odd jobs and I sing in a restaurant once a week.

For fifty pence I can get through the weekend, foodwise: a box of porridge, a quart of milk, a package of tea, some carrots and onions.

DAVID. I've been making tables and saving money. At last, for the first time in my life, I've got enough money to go off somewhere. It's taken all my energy and all my time. Also, I'm very ambivalent about Emma, so I don't know how I feel vis-à-vis another woman. I'm obviously still involved with Emma but I don't want to go back to what we had before and to being what I had become. We were in a tight, unsatisfying relationship—we were treating one another with contempt. At least that isn't happening now. I wish, more than anything, to establish a new peaceful and trustful relationship. To part in enmity would be a dreadful thing.

MARTIN. My home is really my work—working on my designs. It doesn't matter where I do it, a cafe or a library, but I need somewhere to sleep, to wash and to prepare food.

SIMON. At times it has been like a boarding house here—when nobody really wants to know each other.

DAVID. Perhaps I'd just like to travel—meet and know people as I go. I like that. I feel a bit of a romantic about the need to wander. But also, I need sometimes to be creative and I think I am at present.

I don't want any kind of modern trimmings—perhaps a water tap and nothing else. I have been happy in those circumstances, a very simple place in the country, but that doesn't fit in with modern life or children. Life sometimes seems cluttered with people—even in this house I sometimes avoid people. I long for the equilibrium of mind that springs from solitude. This, however, *is* possible here. It is one of the positive qualities.

SIMON. This house evolves and changes very rapidly. I remember being in the kitchen with Sue and things had been very calm and stable for three weeks, and we agreed that it was *boring*. Two days later my ex-wife and our children came to stay here for a time; I sort of moved out and the house went upside down.

MIKE. I don't know why I'm here. I'm confused about it and my possible future; I'm reassessing my position with the other people in the house. Simultaneously there is some antagonism from some quarters and some good vibes from others.

DAVID. I've been self-employed since the children were born so I've been able to devote a lot of time to them. But it's years and years since I had a secure income.

I can get back now from making furniture and feel my time

belongs to me. It's the freest thing I've done—perhaps not the freest, but I don't quite know what else to do. I'd like to balance it with something more cerebral. I believe people should do many different things in their lives. But at the moment that is difficult. I feel making tables out of oak that will last forever is worthwhile—the best thing I have done perhaps. The whole style of making my furniture contradicts everything that is modern and mass-produced. It's crude and strong and made of old oak.

SIMON.   I find it difficult to share everything. I live very frugally, but we middle-class people have possessions as security, and professional incomes, and we learn to plan ahead. Working-class people are much better at living from day to day and therefore they are better at sharing, which is something I respect. I suppose this house follows part of the freak culture which feels that possessions are decorations and luxuries.

DAVID.   My childhood culture was philistine working class aspiring to be vulgar middle class. My parents had many good qualities, tolerance especially, and a certain determination to enjoy life. It is unfortunate perhaps that they did not try to be more themselves. Good-natured working-class get togethers are a high point in my childhood recollection. It is a pity they saw fit to lose so much of it in order to become acceptably middle class. This rubbed off on me, and I took it further. I was a washout at school. Left at fifteen and started work—messenger, clerk, shop assistant, painter, et cetera. I was appalled and incredulous that people could be content to do such boring jobs. I tried to change myself by force. I read all the classics, wrote plays and poems, and I suppose became too precious for the world. I was led to regard western culture with a kind of awe, but in the last ten years (and especially is it exemplified in this house), it all seems to count for very little.

Rock is a powerful force and it is not simply because it is played on loud stereo amplifiers. It is a powerful culture in its own right and is attached to a wholly new style of life, work and relationships. I think it is a good thing and that the establishment has not realized how culturally subversive it is.

I feel subverted, and I feel I must constantly sort through the various theories and lifestyles that are offered to me in order not to be led off down a dark alley. I think by now I might have ended up culturally schizophrenic—having two quite separate cultures vying with one another, neither claiming my entire allegiance. I put down my ability to maintain a degree of synthesis and to be on good terms with a number of culturally diverse people to the fact that I was fortunate enough to have studied philosophy for six years. I have cursed the fact that when I finally managed to get accepted for University College, London, in nineteen sixty-three, (one of the best philosophy departments in the country) I shall have chosen philosophy. It's pretty well useless for getting a job—except teaching, of which I have done quite a bit. But as times goes on I realise that there is something to be said for philosophy for it's own sake. It is a powerful subject which transcends cultures. It has saved me from many a perilous precipice. I would like to do some work of a vaguely philosophical nature again; it would counterbalance my present "old English craftsman" image, which is fun but not really me.

I do think that drugs have made an enormous difference in the world today. I think that head culture is, perhaps, drug-oriented. Combined with that, I think drugs alter these people and make them different, irrevocably different.

SUE.   In rejecting my marriage, when I also doubted the value of all the work we'd done together, I rejected almost all the standards of the conventional world. From then, when I took a step out and started relating to the world from who I really was, it was almost like being a baby again. You question everything all the time. I'm just beginning to accept the validity of some of the standards of the conventional world without having to accept the whole lot of them.

DAVID.   I feel very alienated [if I go into] an ordinary straight pub with straight people drinking their beer. Sometimes I actually feel horror.

Marriage is a straight institution—whether you can alter it and make it into a hip institution I don't know.

ZAPP. This place has given me the space to do what I need to do, space to give, without judgment for achievement or production.

SUE. You could say that my work and creative energies have been very much directed towards the house. When people say, "What are you doing with your life?" I might answer, "I've been trying to find and evolve an alternative family—with the mutual support and warmth of the people living together in this house." I'm in the position in this house of having the power to change things while, relatively, other people haven't. As people have been pointing out recently, this whole house and the way it has gone over the last two and a half years is Sue working out her own life and sorting herself out. But they choose to be here.

I don't think it matters where I'm going; all I want to do is to live my life with a certain integrity. I've got what I want, which is my children. I'm not interested, at the moment in trying to get a sort of "mate" relationship. I've done that, I've been married. The only thing that matters now is to live life in the right kind of way.

Once we had someone here who was very intense. He hated us, he hated the world—he even tried to kill the rabbit. We all found him difficult to live beside. I knew it wasn't an atmosphere I wanted to be in, but I felt it was more important to try and make it into something good than just to say "Go, I can't stand you any more." But in the end, I saw I could no longer live with that hate and that I was getting nowhere in what I was trying to do, so I had to say, "I'm sorry, I no longer want to live in the same house as you, you'll have to go." But I felt an enormous sense of failure that that had to happen.

We do get people who are emotional parasites and financial parasites—it sometimes goes together—people who hang on and take energy out of your life. This is very draining.

We made a deliberate decision that Christmas should be something really good for everyone in this house. We had this vision of everyone's ex-husbands and ex-wives and their children being able to get together, even if just for a meal, that the house should let everyone be together.

Simon dressed in spotless white things and came down looking like a god, with ribbons in his hair and bells on his toes, and sat there smiling and laughing. All these different ways of being were going around this table at the same time and yet it didn't seem to come into conflict. We all seemed to be able to be as we were yet be together.

CHILDREN

SIMON. I discovered my relationship with my children as they grew. I couldn't get involved in the pregnancy—the children were hers. When Jenny was fifteen months old we had a car crash and Carol and Jenny were hurt, and from then on I realized how responsible I was for them.

ZAPP. Until I came to this house, and since childhood, I'd had very little contact with children. I was wary of them—they are terribly bold. But coming to know them and watching, I see so many things that they're into—it's such a pleasure . . . to share experience.

SIMON. I don't think the couple situation works very well with children. Children need attention—when they come to stay here they have Sue's three children and a lot of other people to absorb that need. In a couple situation they appear to want their parents' attention almost continually.

We lived with another couple for a while, but there was friction between the children and jealousy about how we related to each other's children.

DAVID. I have the children here at weekends, which can be quite a strain, but being without them for more than three or four days affects me seriously. This is a problem I don't see how to get around. It's all right after one or two days but I soon miss them. Therefore, it seems Emma and I must remain in the same town until the children are grown up. I feel if they left Brighton, it would be a heartbreaking and radical change for me if I wasn't to see them for three months.

The more I think about it, the more I see there is no real alternative to the family, unless it can be several families sharing an amount of child-care. For the first three years of marriage, it was never possible to go out at night—we could rarely afford a baby-sitter. Then, to feel free, you need to go out on impulse—you don't want to arrange it a week ahead, do you?

If I wanted to go away with Emma now, to work things out between us, we'd have to take the children and that would probably mess everything up.

I can bring the children here and they sleep in my room with me. I can see the difference in Emma after she has been relieved of the children for two days. She is worn out on Friday night and on Sunday she is relaxed and warm. She used to be so lively and a powerful personality. Now she has become subdued and marred by shouting at the children.

SIMON. I often find the children a nuisance. I sometimes feel that what they care about is their home and to a large extent the other people living in the house are peripheral. Unless someone were to damage her children, Sue doesn't see it as her responsibility how the children and grown-ups relate. She just lets it happen. The same goes for the relationships among the children—the adults don't interfere. They are all very free here and that's how Sue wants it.

SUE. I felt intuitively that the children needed other adults around them and that it wouldn't be right for me to go off and live in a remote part of the country alone with them. I felt that what I should be doing was trying to get a bigger nuclear family together around us, and this was a healthy way to be. I've mostly had people around me who are nice to the children and can relate to them, and I think that's important—for them to be familiar with other adults who have different attitudes and ideas.

MARTIN. I've found living with the children very valuable. I used to be uneasy with children. I've learned to let go, to be open to their crazy games, their warmth and spontaneity, how they immediately express their disapproval or approval. I've learned to love them I suppose.

SUE. I'm confused about education, because I can see some value in what they're doing at school and I don't know that I should take them away from an "establishment" school. I'm much more concerned with attitudes and ways of relating to the world than I am with information. I feel that if they can relate to the world in a basically healthy way, that is, from their own center, then acquiring knowledge will come easily. I think it's important for children to learn about basic survival. I don't mean so much in the physical sense, although that has to go with it, but survival in the sense that if they want to find out about how to make a guinea-pig cage, they know how to get the information and use it.

I feel that children need love and emotional security and opportunities and, after that, the organism—that is, the child—will look after itself.

SEX AND LOVE

SUE. I feel I no longer need the protective element from a man. I'm not looking for that, partly because I've still got it with Peter —he provides shelter and money and a certain share of the responsibility of the children. By the same token, I don't need the economic things. What I seem to need now is friendship, emotional and sexual empathy and closeness, a relationship in which I can grow emotionally, feel secure emotionally, so I can get on with other aspects of my life.

In my relationship with Mike we keep many parts of our lives quite separate. Sometimes we do things with the children, but he doesn't come right in on my relationship with them—there's no routine. Fortunately he has the same hang-ups about not getting coupled—we don't have meals together, we need to feel we each have elbowroom. He has a self-contained flat in the basement, and I find this a freedom that works for the time being.

I like to be able to walk out of the door not saying to anyone when I'll be back. I even have problems about a double bed—I suppose because it smacks of marriage. We couldn't sleep in a double bed for ages—it really freaked me out.

MIKE. I found living in a couple very limiting—there just wasn't enough space for spontaneity. I don't think two people have the same rhythms, and if they are forced to cohabit the same mental space continually—with no one else except the children—it can only end in a repressive situation. But I don't see any real alternative.

SUE. My relationship with Mike is complicated. We've taken a lot of time to ourselves, we've needed it. This has involved periods of not spending a lot of time with other people in the house and not spending enough time with the children. I need to be alone with myself some part of every day, and this I do quite ruthlessly. Nowadays I'm quite disciplined about how I spend time each day, parceling it out on this and that. I know that if I don't give myself that balance for my varying needs, everything starts going wrong and I can't deal with any part of it constructively.

MIKE. Sensuality is the bridge between Sue and me—sometimes it holds, sometimes it doesn't. Any sexual relationship needs time, and sometimes I feel Sue's life is very departmentalized, with the children and the other people in the house. Perhaps if everyone was involved in a mutual sexuality, it could be very happy. But I doubt it.

SIMON. In my head and my fantasy, ideally, I'd like to find "the woman"—but I don't expect to. Ideally I believe in romantic love, but it is limiting and it does preclude close exploration of other relationships. And still I'd choose it. I don't see why one shouldn't find more independence with someone to come back to. During the last years of my marriage we both became acutely aware that we needed our separate lives and our separate activities, but because we were insecure about the marriage we spent all our time together.

DAVID. I think there is something wrong about marriage. Even without children I think marriage would destroy a relationship —it takes away the "romantic affair" aspect which, when contained in the marriage, goes wrong. The falling in love goes beyond the children. Children confirm the marriage and the roles become firmly set.

ZAPP. I can imagine living in a couple situation but I'm not sure for how long—I think it would be too enclosed for me. I need freedom as I need love.

Sometimes it is difficult here not to get caught up in someone else's "bad times" to the extent of becoming very depressed oneself. But we can only learn through situations to come to terms with other people's experience.

I feel I do get nourishment but I'm not sure if my needs for emotional nourishment are completely satisfied. At times we have a lot of stimulus from outside; we seem to be part of a network where other people are also searching.

MARTIN. Moving around so much, I haven't made any roots. I have a great itchy-footedness—I want to travel, yet I haven't got the credentials for travel. I haven't a flair for making friends, I'm overshy and I pretend to myself I don't need friends.

ZAPP. Best for me is that here I've been given the space to develop and mature. At the same time there are warmth and caring and children around. I think that we are blessed to have such a place and to be together in it.

SUE. I think I would never want to formally get married again because it seems to put external limits on your relationship, partly through conditioned ideas of what a marriage should be, and partly because of the external structures of marriage—like the idea of being committed to someone for ever and ever. This can come into conflict with genuine honesty in your relationship because if you're committed for ever and ever to the idea of marriage, it's difficult at any point to say this isn't working. So I hesitate to get into marriage again because I believe that the most important thing about any relationship is to be very honest, to help each other to be honest.

One of the new and exciting things about my relationship with Mike is that we're very flexible about roles and we can both move along the masculine-feminine line in quite a balanced way. We are not hung up into thinking he's got to do man things and I've got to do woman things. Even emotionally we can change around quite freely.

Perhaps, till now, I have related to all the men in the house as a husband. I've hated taking decisions and dealing with the outside world over things like plumbers—I find it difficult to acknowledge that the tap's even dripping, let alone get someone to fix it—I want a man to do it. It's almost as if I've cast Peter out of fulfilling all those roles and set up another husband with seven different bodies—it often feels like that.

There have been women living in the house, but only much younger ones. Then I have been a mother. It's no accident that there hasn't been another woman with children living here—I suppose I'm not ready to move over, be a sister, drop this super-woman myth I'm playing out. I've never had a sexual relationship with a man who needs a wife—it's almost as if I have to keep sex away from being a wife. I have a very good relationship with the men on their own. They come home and tell me about their awful days and their emotional hassles, et cetera. Sex has never come into it, although there is a sort of sexual vibe going on. This is where it's interesting with Mike, because when I met him it was a purely sexual, emotional thing and I kept him right out of the husband trip. I didn't let him get involved with the children or my day-to-day life at all, and it's just gradually getting nearer. Now he's moved into the house, but only into the self-contained basement.

The children seem to have responded to Mike's being in my life without much trauma, perhaps because he's clearly been "Mom's friend" and not an alternative Dad. Also they're accustomed to many men intertwined in their lives. Mike responds to them as a person, a friend. We hardly ever do anything together as a family unit.

POLITICS

DAVID. One of the good things about this house is Sue's eccentricity. It's not based on some high-minded theory about how people should live.

MARTIN. I'm dedicated to making some good changes in the world. My main concern is the use of solar energy on a big scale.

I also feel concerned about the high standard of living everyone expects—people sink into a comfortable frame of mind where a lot of talking about changes goes on but nothing is ever done.

It's a hard world where we are no longer allowed to build ourselves a shelter to live in but always have to pay rent—if I have to pay every week for a space then it's not really mine. A space that's really mine would be a space I didn't have to pay for every week, but that I could build once and for all.

SUE. When I was at the point of rejecting everything, marriage and the straight world and all the values I'd lived by, I realized that political action is not the important thing. The important thing is people getting to know themselves and relating to everybody else. Political action seems to me to ignore that and deal with the external structures in the outside world and forget people's centers. Taking responsibility away from people and creating political structures for them—this can often hinder people in finding their own centers and taking responsibility for their own lives.

If you can relate to the world in such a way as to help people find their own centers and take responsibility for their own integrity, this is helping things grow from a healthy ground, and the external structures will then look after themselves and be a true reflection of needs.

WHERE TO?

SIMON. We are beginning to share our endeavors but somehow we don't see ourselves as building anything permanent here. We are trying to find out how to support ourselves.

My dream is of an extended family in the country from which I can come and go. I feel I want a group of people I can relate to as a family—perhaps it's childishness but I don't want to feel alone in the world. I feel a bit like a cat who likes it's own private territory to return to but goes out and wanders.

SUE. The house has always been for people in transition, who don't know where they are and have been broken in some way and are trying to get together. We have been helping each other find ourselves and then move outwards.

POSTSCRIPT

SIMON. The first law is movement, evolution. The first priority flows from the children. The center of this house is that it exists as a home for Ben, Clara and Lucinda, and now, through their needs, my needs, our needs, extending to embrace Jenny and Jake. That is the first meaning of this house. Round this are elaborated the many themes of our lives.

The house changed fundamentally at the time of these interviews. Until that time the house was a collection of isolated spirits camped in a Victorian dwelling of medium size, eleven rooms, attic, kitchen and bathrooms. Shared space was semislum. For me it was a very frustrating place to be. Every other day I would cast my mind to leaving—nothing was happening—but what potential!

With Mike's arrival the balance of the household shifted fundamentally. It began to become a home for Sue.

The day after Nell's first visit, Mike and I "shooed" Martin from the house. Money was a symptom. Martin's needs we felt to be a large distraction and drain and tension. I felt that trying to accommodate him jeopardized the things I desired for the house. As we were, there was no progress to be made. We needed a break, a holiday.

The essential fulcrum of the spring's rebalance was Sue's departure from the house. It allowed me to mend the three-months-broken ground floor window—landlady's responsibility? It allowed us to build the new kitchen. This creation of the house's hearth was, incidentally, Mike's conception, though realized by all of us, and David in particular. I'm sure it was only Mike's special relationship to Sue that allowed us to dare to start on the kitchen without her explicit consent, though when she left she left us a pretty free hand.

With Sue away, Mike was able to relate to the rest of us directly, rather than as Sue's boyfriend.

So, anyway, during the two weeks that Sue was away we were able to make the house our home; and with this reshuffling of our relationships, Sue then felt able to return, not as landlady matriarch, but into a more brotherly-sisterly nexus.

And so we had a summer discovering bonds and affection as a household. Bob has returned to us. Mike ventures with a workshop (for us). Mike and Sue built the kiln last winter, before Mike's arrival in the house. The kiln, however, has not been used, but waits—our energies are elsewhere scattered, not yet galvanized. We speak of moving to the country and continue our preparations, which are primarily a matter of getting on with the business of living—becoming an extended family.

Now, this autumn, we have embarked on another great upheaval and adventure. Carol, my ex-wife, Jenny and Jake have joined the household, and to accommodate this I have in part moved out. How courageous is my sister Sue. And so we move and grow.

ZAPP. We teach each other as we learn.

SUE. We're a tree. The household's the trunk. Different people, different needs, a solid body which (amazingly) grows. Smoothly, with tangles, laughter, anguish, we grow. The roots are the children. The sap is the love between us all.

Branches grew this last summer, like our cherished garden. The pottery was born, but now is dormant, waiting for its moment. Mike and David have a workshop each, making elegant solid furniture from wood which would otherwise be burned. A small theater group flowered exotically. An alternative school wants to emerge.

Inside the trunk we're quivering gently under the shock of a change-around. Bob has come home, Carol and her two children are welcomed, Mike and I have conceded our "individuality" and are living together.

It feels a lot cleaner, less cluttered inside the trunk now. I often feel a light shining around and within us. It's very awesome.

MIKE. Help!

I loved the Bohemianism of Brighton—Sue's courage in her search for freedom and herself; how she didn't try to control what happened in the house; the way I could arrive and sleep under the rafters with the wind rattling the slates, my head inside my sleeping bag, cracks of sky showing when I took it out.

Back home Dan and I moved the bed out of my room down into the sitting room. Now we get undressed in front of the fire, drop our clothes on the floor. Some kind of return to student digs life?

We have a curfew on our new home. No children are allowed in after 9:30 at night. I can be a free woman, lie naked on the sofa dropping grapes into my mouth if that's what I fancy. Our room is our shared territory—we each have a room of our own if we want to be alone or sleep alone. Our life is developing; I think we are both learning from this book.

I am also learning to accept that I hate housekeeping and cooking. I am no longer ashamed of doing both badly. And just occasionally, when I don't have to do them, I enjoy them all.

What was most difficult in our threesome was the social situation. People took sides, either for me or for Nicole; they couldn't accept us as together by choice. They became very chauvinistic; they'd say, "Oh, life's all right for John—he's got two chicks." But this wasn't true. If anything, his problems were the greatest. And I think it was courageous of him to try to live with two women.

7. SHARING A MAN: NICOLE, JOHN AND ROSE

It is difficult to give a clear picture of Nicole, John and Rose because soon after I had met them and Tina had photographed them, Nicole left. So the story is more about the failure of three people to sustain an open sexual relationship, for Nicole and Rose to share John sexually. Perhaps John wasn't enough of a superman—who knows? However, I wanted to include them although they no longer exist as a threesome—they are a genuine part of the revolt against coupledom. They are also of that same generation, in their late twenties and early thirties, which is resisting the nuclear family but haven't yet found a viable alternative.

John and Nicole were both students doing advanced degree

courses, having worked, in John's case, for several years. Rose has a highly responsible job. When I first met her, and the three of them were living together, Rose said, "It's nicer to come home to two people. **99**

WHERE FROM?

ROSE. I see my parents as incredibly self-contained within themselves—they have virtually no social contact whatsoever. They have no real friends; nothing new has come into their lives for years and they haven't provided stimulation for each other.

I've always been happiest with lots of people around me, like student houses. I was never lonely—there was always someone there. In the couple situation people can become neurotically dependent.

I think there are times when two people can be just as lonely as one, no matter how loving and close they are. I was pleased when Nicole moved in, really pleased.

JOHN. I feel very aware of the pressure and paranoid about the expectations of being in a couple. I felt guilty when I was bored— I'd start thinking, Are we not suited?

NICOLE. Rose and John were lovers and then Rose went away to university. John and I were at university together and I started sleeping with him; he went off at odd weekends to visit Rose and then she came down to London and I met her. It was a bit strange. We had supper together in their flat and we all pretended the situation was quite normal and I was coming to supper with friends. This situation went on for some time and I imagined John would either split from Rose or it would finish between him and me, but neither happened.

Rose came back from university and so the three of us were

all in the flat, and we decided to live as a threesome. It seemed an exciting idea.

NOW

JOHN. It was Rose who suggested the sharing of me.

NICOLE. At first nobody was too sure about who would be sleeping where. That was uncomfortable and we'd sit up late into the night looking at each other.

JOHN. There were tensions at first as nobody quite knew where they were.

NICOLE. We decided to sleep alternate nights with John and that went on O.K. till we had some terrific bust-up. Rose had been away for the weekend, to give me time on my own with John as she'd been with him three or four years and knew him much better. Anyway, when she came back, he let slip to her that we had screwed four times in one afternooon, and she got very jealous and resentful that I was, as it were, taking it all and that when he came to sleep with her he would be sated.

So we decided it should be two nights each, so that when he'd had his tremendous amount of screwing with me, he could then get over it on the first night and have a good night on the second night.

ROSE. I was very hurt when some of my friends seemed to imply that Nicole should supersede me—that I should step back. Then I began to feel very jealous. Before that I had enjoyed coming home and finding Nicole there, and her friends coming round enriched my life. We even talked about the long term and we were very optimistic.

As far as the domestic chores went, it was good. There was less to do with three to share it. We started gardening, at Nicole's suggestion, and it was more fun cooking for three.

JOHN. When I first slept with Rose, four and a half years ago, she was a virgin. So I encouraged her to sleep with other men—if we were going to stay together, I knew I couldn't be the only man she'd slept with all her life. I was never jealous about her screwing other people. Perhaps there's something wrong with me and I should, but I don't feel jealousy, I really don't.

NICOLE. Sometimes I felt that I was being used to ease the relationship—to supply stimulus—and the fact that Rose felt threatened seemed an unnecessary strain on me.

JOHN. Nicole set higher standards for her relationship with me than she did for her relationship with Rose, which I thought was a pity and a pressure on me.

ROSE. We had too little space in the flat. We only had one big room, which was the living room where John slept, and one small bedroom where Nicole or I slept when we were alone.

I think one's own private space is very important. A room each would have made a lot of difference and made both Nicole and me less dependent on John.

JOHN. I used to wake up in the night sometimes and wonder who was there and find out by feeling.

SEX AND LOVE

JOHN. It was somehow assumed that I didn't have any problems, and therefore, it was usually me sitting down with Rose or Nicole to listen to their feelings about *their* relationship with me, rather than the other way around. I once read in the paper about three women who were taken to court by a man for raping him. They were found guilty but the judge made lots of sexist remarks like, "I'm sure there are lots of men who'd like to be in your position," and he only fined them a farthing. Of course the situation was enjoyable for me, but it was not without its problems and responsibilities.

NICOLE. When John was sleeping with Rose I'd feel very left out if they stayed in bed for ages in the morning. Sometimes, if I knew they'd just been screwing, it could make me feel very insecure.

JOHN. Sometimes I wanted to get up early at the weekends, but I couldn't because the one I was in bed with would say, "You're getting up early because you're with me, but when you're with her you lie in!"

ROSE. I became obsessed with the fact that Nicole entered the relationship with a strong preference for John, and that she tolerated rather than accepted me. The nights John was sleeping with Nicole, I used to feel lonely, and sometimes jealous, because Nicole very markedly wanted John and I was superfluous at those times. I felt excluded. I would have slept with them, but Nicole was nervous that if John had screwed us both in the same bed it would have got competitive.

JOHN. I sometimes felt that the situation was viewed in a rather hostile way by other people, so that whatever might happen, I would never have got any sympathy, but only my "just deserts."

ROSE. I did consider having other lovers, partly because a man can't really satisfy two women sexually. Ideally, if there is a three-way relationship, it should be bisexually, among the three. I am bisexual, but it never happened between Nicole and me, though I hoped that with time it might have.

NICOLE. I never felt sympathetic towards the idea of the three of us sleeping together, though I have actually slept with another couple—both of whom I knew individually, which wasn't the case with Rose, whom I got to know through John.

There is some aspect of their sexuality which I object to. I felt that if I was involved in a triangular sexual scene with both of them, John would be enjoying it in a salacious way—so it repelled me, sleeping with them together.

JOHN. I didn't usually have any preference about who I was going to sleep with and I didn't want to be seen to favor one. Sometimes the "sleeping rota" didn't coincide with who I'd been out with in the evening, but I just took that in my stride as part of it. Sometimes they each had the impression that I was seeing the other or screwing the other more, and they'd get at me separately. I think it was pretty even myself.

ROSE. Sometimes I felt sorry at having less opportunity for intimate talks with John but I hoped that would be made up for by a close relationship with Nicole. Unfortunately she was more interested in getting close to John, so sometimes I felt I'd lost out.

NICOLE. Once we went away to the country for the weekend and we went on a walk. They were walking ahead, talking animatedly, and I was overwhelmed by an agonizing jealousy for the first time and realized how much I had been repressing.

JOHN. It would have been much better if everybody had been bisexual and all three of our relationships were equally involved.

ROSE. The idea was not to live with John on his own, because I think two people can be as lonely as one. There comes a point of stagnation, where you think too much the same, you get too absorbed in each other's problems.

JOHN. Most people feel so guilty about their sexual relationships when they are outside the norm. They resented my apparent lack of guilt.

ROSE. It was as if our friends couldn't accept that John's relationship with both Nicole and me was serious. They can accept screwing around if it's not serious, but they couldn't quite take our living together.

JOHN. I resented any implication that I was exploiting the girls— I had no magic power over them, they were both free.

ROSE. What was most difficult in our threesome was the social situation. People took sides, either for me or for Nicole; they couldn't accept us as together by choice. They became very chauvinistic; they'd say, "Oh, life's all right for John—he's got two chicks." But this wasn't true. If anything, his problems were the greatest. And I think it was courageous of him to try to live with two women.

JOHN. I went down to see my parents once and it struck me that it was the first night I'd had on my own, without sexual expectations, for four months, and how nice it was.

I don't see myself as having children, for the next three or four years anyway, though I may one day regret not having had them. I think they make it harder to lead a full social life, but some people use them as an excuse to do almost nothing.

ROSE. Even children don't fit within a couple. They often don't enrich coupledom; sometimes they even make it more cramping. For many they become objects that stop you going out and stop you having time to yourself.

I don't find it enough just to screw outside people—I don't get involved in their lives. I see living with people as a totally different experience. Also, friends see you as a couple and don't make friends with you as an individual, whereas in the living situation, you relate as yourself.

The three of us used to go out together in the hope that friends wouldn't see us as rivals. But I think people saw my relationship with John as the dying one and his relationship with Nicole as the growing one. So few people can make the leap to see people as individuals.

THE END . . . AND THE FUTURE

NICOLE. At the end everything happened so quickly. I felt that John didn't want the kind of serious involvement that I wanted; he wanted something completely spontaneous—he didn't want to 'talk' about it. I felt very lacking in confidence and he wouldn't face it. That night, I was sleeping with John but I lay awake, realizing I either had to accept the situation or I had to go. And I suddenly thought, There's a whole world outside, I don't have to accept what's not making me happy. I can leave and live and enjoy myself—I only have to leave this flat. The next morning I packed my things and I went around the flat saying good-bye to the room and the garden. I didn't say anything to John—it was as if I was in a dream—and finally I drifted off home. My mother was there and I said, "I've left the flat," and she said, "Great, you can come home and live here."

ROSE. It came as an awful shock when Nicole left. It happened so suddenly—we both felt we'd been jilted. It was traumatic.

JOHN. I was very upset about Nicole leaving; I didn't think it was going to break up. Rose and I both felt communally jilted—it was a very odd feeling. I walked around the house crying and saying it would never be the same again.

NICOLE. I felt tremendously upset. When I saw John a day or two later, I asked him to leave Rose and come to me, and he refused. That was the end of it.

JOHN. I'd certainly be prepared to try a threesome again. I believe there are people who are happier living in unconventional ways, and I'm one of them.

ROSE. I don't feel upset when John sleeps with other people or when we are apart. I know there is always someone to go back to. Our relationship has benefited from contact with other people.

JOHN. I suppose I screwed Rose more when Nicole left.

ROSE. Now Nicole has gone, I'd like to try living with other people again. I try to travel a lot on my own—I find it necessary to get away from this couple mentality. I need to be involved with other people; my ideal would be four or six people living and sleeping together, interrelating.

JOHN. I think if I had children I'd like to bring them up communally with other people, partly because I wouldn't want them as a tie. I don't see myself as a great parent—although I like to keep the options open.

I feel you have to get the adult life worked out very carefully first. I spent a lot of time trying to sort out and be in touch with Nicole and Rose. Finally, I felt closer, more in touch with Rose —that's why I stayed when Nicole left.

POSTSCRIPT

A year later, over home-brewed champagne and hot chestnuts.

JOHN. Do we really want this to sound so negative? You two make it sound as though it had been hell!

NICOLE. All the bad bits seem so irrevelant now. There were so many good times as well—the New Year disco and the Halloween party, and all those suppers we had at home together.

JOHN. I make it that Nicole has put in one factual statement and ten complaints.

NICOLE. But for me the situation was "given." It was a learning one; I wasn't developing my own ideas about relationships, but learning from yours. I'm only beginning to appreciate it now.

ROSE. I feel that the satisfaction from our domestic life has been understated. We talked to you about the problems, but there was a whole relaxed side to our life—where we got into vegetarianism and being at home and talking—that brought a lot of happiness. I really liked those evenings when we were all at home.

NICOLE. We did offer him the single bed, but he couldn't bear the thought of Rose and me sleeping without him so he turned it down!

JOHN. Forget all the pretence about it being hard work—it was marvelous!

' *I ask myself what I feel about monogamy and unfaithfulness and multiple relationships.*

At the moment I choose to be sexually involved with only one person. Perhaps I shouldn't even say I choose? I feel open to the possibility of others, but it doesn't happen; so I'm faithful and it rather amazes me but I like it.

I also feel that the agony of sexual jealousy is, perhaps for most people, the most acute pain suffered. Nevertheless, I think I'd choose to "suffer" in order to be free sexually. 🙶

Six years ago, everything Martin did impinged on me. Now I have my own farm—I am always so busy.

8. THE COUPLE: MARTIN AND ROSIE

I wanted to include Murren Farm, however briefly, partly for a breath of country air in the middle of this mostly urban book, and partly because I don't want to completely damn marriage or "the couple."

Martin and Rosie are married and yet they live a completely unconventional life. The only routine is feeding the animals. When I was there, Rosie sat by the fire plucking some geese while Martin made supper, and later she dried the feathers in the oven to make pillows. Other people with kids live on the hillside. Their lives interweave; the children sleep in each others houses, share each other's food and toys. The adults also interact to a large extent.

Rosie has found a way of escaping typical motherhood and housewifery, but not by employing a nanny and going out to work. Instead she has done it by making a life for herself on the premises but outside the house. The children, knowing she is about, don't need her in the house—most things they can do for themselves and in emergencies they can find her.

Murren stands on a hill above Kington. The house is like an ever-growing wooden mushroom, built by Martin (who is a builder). As an extra room or stable or sty is needed, so it appears.

It all faces onto an old walled garden, which Martin was given by his parents, and where Rosie now grows her vegetables and food for her animals.

They have five children—Michael, thirteen, Sophie, twelve, Elizabeth, ten, Francis, nine, and Polly, three. Polly is particularly keen on farming but was, unfortunately, away at the time helping her uncle run his farm.

All the animals are free-ranging and so are the children. By this I mean the children have remarkably few rules or expectations laid on them. They don't have to help with the animals if they don't want to, nor do they have to help around the kitchen. At the same time, if they want ironed clothes for school on Monday morning or a cooked breakfast, they have to do it for themselves.

Martin and Rosie have a beautiful room, with a log fire and a sofa at one end and a bed and a phonograph and Martin's filing system at the other, and books all the way round. This room is kept sacred; otherwise the children do what they like in the rest of the house. The only shared room is the kitchen, where everyone eats and argues and laughs. And where Elizabeth told me, "It's like living in the Stone Age here—it's awful!"

Economically the setup works because Martin is a builder— they couldn't make enough money to survive on just thirty-six acres, or so far they haven't. Rosie hopes it might happen one day.

I feel they are an inspiration to their children. That sounds pretentious and Rosie would never say something like that. Rosie says, "I'd rather be out on the farm than doing all the things mothers are 'meant' to do."

Physically, it's quite a hard life, in the way that farming traditionally is: out in all weathers, mud on the kitchen floor, sick animals to sit up with at night. And of course it ties them down —a cow can't be left to milk herself, even when Polly says, "But we've got plenty of milk, Mom! **99**

MARTIN. I suppose I believe that everything you possess you should use. If, like I do, you have a wife who loves getting her head down in the pig bucket, then you have an answer to the life here. And if the children don't have a mother who washes their clothes much or who doesn't appear at the kitchen sink, they can at least see her as a person who is working at something that enlarges their lives.

To be single-minded about life is quite an impressive thing, but it also tends to be narrow, and people like that miss a lot. The object, for me, is to be a kind of mist, a broad mist that gets into all the corners of life. Really, what is interesting about human beings is that they can change shape all the time and discover so many different things, in life and in themselves. The possibilities are enormous.

There must be some logic about the life you lead, but not a knifelike logic. You get this from mixed farming, where you have animals relating to each other, which on many farms never happens. For example, if you keep a pig in a sty and a chicken gets into the sty, the pig will eat it; whereas if they are both free ranging, the chicken will sit on the back of the pig eating lice, with the pig grunting in pleasure.

We like being part of this cycle which relates to our own life and death. It seems to me this experience is an enlargement of our own lives.

ROSIE. I feel guilty about being privileged. So I feel at least if I can grow the food and someone else hasn't got to do it for me, I feel less guilty.

Six years ago, everything Martin did impinged on me. Now I have my own farm—I am always so busy.

If you have animals you can get almost ill from worry about looking after them. You can't sleep at night if one of them is ill.

I spend a lot of time in plotting ways to get the animals to look after themselves better. I've got a fixation about this mother and baby scene—I can't bear babies being parted from mothers at all. I think animals can be psychologcally damaged by it. I've seen foster calves almost die in the field from being separated from their mothers.

Most of the children aren't very interested, but I hope they'll have absorbed some of it when they grow up.

It's this rotten mother syndrome—if you haven't got your head hung over the kitchen sink all day, you're a rotten mother. Well, I couldn't bear all that. So now at least I'm here when they come home from school—I'm physically on the place. I'm probably not in the kitchen making cocoa for them, but I'm probably milking the cow and it's that milk they can make their own cocoa with.

I think children shouldn't be so apart from the work as they are in the industrial society. Children never see their parents working, they're never a part of the work, they're never asked to contribute at all. Whereas with farming, they can do a lot, such as feeding calves. They really can be a terrific help and understand how it all works.

I went to Francis's school to an open house and I read in his diary for October third, "Mom's cow had her calf yesterday and Mom has to milk the two front tits and the calf sucks the two back tits." So at least it gives him something to write in his diary!

At one moment we suggested we might go and live in Bath for six months, thinking the children would love to be in town for a while, but none of them would come. "No, we want to stay here in our own home," they said furiously.

It's a great privilege to have thirty-six acres. It's an unattainable goal for most people. I don't like large farms at all. I'd like

an awful lot more people in England to have ten acres each—
enough to be self-sufficient on. I think the land would improve
enormously.

There is so much satisfaction to be got out of a small farm. I
particularly like the animals being born.

" *Coming away from Murren, I know how much I miss the country. Those still, magic, soundless, empty and misty landscapes.
Soft air on my cheek. Time slowing down. Lying on the grass
talking to friends. The thin shouts of happy children in the distance. Why then do I live in the city? I don't have to.*

*I need both, but perhaps I need the city more. I need the un-
expectedness, the sense of adventure the city gives me. I like the
cosmopolitan feel of it all and I like the late night shops and
cinemas. Best of all, I like, need, love my friends. I want a base
in the city with the freedom to visit and travel, to go out into the
country.* "

The continual struggle to free ourselves from internalized parents—which I luke to be a part of all our experience—seems to become even more stressful and complex in the communal group. So many potential parental and sibling relationships.

9. A COMMUNE: RAMSGATE

'The people involved in the Ramsgate commune are:

Peter, who teaches art and English and is a part-time artist and printmaker. He was married to Maureen.

Christine, who is involved with Peter, she teaches children and adults with learning problems.

Maureen, who makes jewelry and was married to Peter. She has now left and lives nearby with John.

Martine, who is French and works for International Community and makes crafts.

Tina, who is half Greek and half French, doing voluntary social work and studying sociology.

Brian, who when I went to Ramsgate was going through a withdrawal and therefore didn't feel like talking much (though he showed me a beautiful photograph of his grandfather, who was a blacksmith, outside his smithy).

Fiona, who had run the play group and was a translator.

Ian, who teaches and comes from the Ramsgate area.

Reuben, eight years old, son of Peter and Maureen; Lea, three, daughter of Tina; Tanya six, daughter of Fiona.

The house is enormous, almost elegant, but somehow slightly too thin, deep and high. A Regency seaside villa with an iron balcony and a tiny backyard, a stone's throw from the beach.

Everyone shares the mortgage—it had been very cheap—and living there is economical but spacious. Everyone cooks in turns and eats together in the evening, usually a large and delicious meal with lots of fresh vegetables from the garden plot.

The people are serious-minded, interested in the arts and education, and experimental in their attitude toward life. For a while they had kept a Book of Dreams, where each morning whoever wanted to could write down his dream of the night before. This was a marvelous book, full of wild, violent, naked dreams; but it had been discontinued because reading the disturbing feelings that came to people during sleep had been painful.

It occurred to me at Ramsgate, as at Brighton and Leeds, that I envied these women who were able to live among other intelligent women, an opportunity the heterosexual woman bringing up children in the nuclear family doesn't have.

However, it also occurred to me at Ramsgate that, because of sexual tangles, there were bad feelings which hadn't been worked through. There was pain and anger which wasn't expressed, almost as if a decision had been taken to let things be, to give up on "getting closer." Too much had been taken on and not enough resolved.

However, I respected their approach to life and liked the way people were welcomed round the fire. 99

WHERE FROM?

PETER. The motivation for setting up this household was to build on the relationship that was already going between Maureen, Christine, myself and Reuben. It seemed right to move into a larger house that would have room for others and thereby make a greater distance between myself and Maureen. And yet would make it possible for Reuben to grow up with all three of us. We chose Ramsgate because we could get a big cheap house near the sea.

Before we moved here, Maureen and I were based in London and we had begun having relationships outside our marriage. There was a breakthrough time when Christine became accepted into our house, but it was not really satisfactory.

MAUREEN. I believed in the monogamous marital relationship but was having to learn and accept the change in Peter and try not to split Reuben's feelings towards us as his parents. My other relationships with men were an effort to find another monogamous, stable pattern, but I met so many unsuitable candidates that I kept coming back to accept the situation at base camp. Christine was tolerated by me always because she was another human being, and, out of respect for Peter's feelings I glossed over what I really felt. She stayed for the occasional meal, usually with another friend, and once or twice at night, which I tried to ignore but soon stopped, as the close proximity was injurious to all concerned. Peter and Christine were in love; he did not want to leave Reuben and me, so what could I do? Tolerate when one felt strong and well and blow up when one felt tired and lonely.

Peter and I never slept together after Reuben's first birthday. We had separate bedrooms, and he wrote me letters about his feelings, as he could not do it, or did not have time, in words. I felt guilty of being an obstacle to his future happiness and, falsely heroic, thought it better if one of us was happy at least, rather than two miserable beings. But he wanted me included in his new life as well. If we had not had Reuben, this would not have happened—I would have left, never entertaining the idea of communal living.

My marriage with Peter broke down, I think, because I wasn't intellectually a sufficient companion for him. I didn't have an intellectual background—brought up in Guernsey, on a farm in Dorset and West of Eire, without books, stimulating schools or aware parents. I was a late starter in appreciating anything in the cultural field; it's taken me ages to catch up.

Perhaps one of the reasons I went into the commune in the first place is that I'd lost the confidence of thinking I could support myself (in a flat) financially. At first Peter and I were getting a divorce and I had very mixed feelings about Christine. I kept myself very separate, upstairs in the house. I was teaching. I found that Reuben was being torn by the fact that I was living upstairs and the rest of the commune and Peter were below, and I thought, Why not join them? At the time the people in the commune weren't really the right people for me. Christine came here starry-eyed and put a lot of energy in, but she hasn't really been repaid. I think it has attracted a lot of inhibited people. A successful commune needs more extrovert people and perhaps a common aim; otherwise it becomes a glorified guesthouse with no one extending themselves to each other.

CHRISTINE.   I was living in London, teaching disturbed children, when my relationship with Peter began.

When we came here I was very idealistic. I had a lot of high hopes, but I was prepared for it not to be easy straightaway. I thought it takes time to build relationships and settle in the locality. I wanted us to have a firm basis and then go on exploring alternatives—alternatives to society, alternatives to the family, a more communal tribal life—although it started on the simple basis of wanting to find a way where the three of us, me, Peter, and Maureen, would be together (though I knew Maureen was ambivalent). I wouldn't have begun a relationship with Peter without my own assurance that love isn't limited, so that it can include several people and that no one person can except to be all and everything to any other one. The diversities of people are endless. Given that Maureen and Peter felt similarly—they didn't want to be bound by laws—granted that basis, and yet wanting to expand more, and feeling that group living was a viable alternative to the family—especially my own feeling that more heads, more hands, more feet would mean more energy—this was a key thing for me. And it was a real blow to me when I realized it didn't mean that.

At first I thought, Never mind, when we get to know each other better, it'll be better later. We're bound to find it hard at first. Then at one point I realized it wasn't and wouldn't be and that I wasn't the kind of person I thought I was, and that the other people weren't the kind of people I'd hoped for. From time to time I've felt disappointed, and at one point I felt it was just awful—it produced turbulence and turmoil inside my own head and I had dreadful depression. It was the first time since I was about twenty that I had had this kind of blackness, a feeling that nothing was worthwhile. And eventually I could articulate that I didn't believe in anything, and after a period of that time, feeling awful in myself, I began to recognize what was awful about outside too, and what I should take action about and not tolerate.

MARTINE. Looking at my parents' life, I realized when I was quite young that I was not going to have that. My father was bored, my mother was dissatisfied! My ideas of a commune involved many more people and more children. I certainly didn't want to re-create the family pattern.

My boyfriend was moving in with me. In fact he'd gone ahead, and then when I arrived, he wasn't there—he left a note to say he'd gone back to his wife. At the time Peter was living here with his wife, Maureen; Christine, his girlfriend; and Reuben, Peter and Maureen's son. There was much tension between them.

Then I started sleeping with Peter, but the balance wasn't right and it was heavy for him.

FIONA. My marriage was very inhibited; we soon realized we wanted more freedom and worked hard to get a commune started with friends. I left when I realized that my husband was very involved with someone else and wasn't giving energy to the group or to the marriage. I felt that however well a couple might get on, I didn't like the possessiveness and the dependence of marriage. Even if you don't want to be dependent, everything makes you so, particularly if you have a child. Everything throws you together, isolates you from other people. You always turn to each other for support and company; you can't talk to other people when things are going wrong because it's considered disloyal and, without quite knowing why, you find yourself in the most awful trap.

I think, in the commune, we are all discontented people. Whatever way we lived we'd find something wrong with it.

BRIAN. I come from a small village somewhere in the middle of Kent. I play the harmonica and the violin.

IAN. I was born and bred near Ramsgate.

TINA. I lived mainly in Mediterranean countries as a child. My parents live in Africa. Lea's father is English. I don't really have any roots anywhere.

I need a stable setup for my daughter, Lea, and have tried the nuclear family and another commune in France.

When I feel secure here, it is because I feel intellectually understood. I have formed a couple of close friendships after living here a year and a half. I still feel it's a pity at times that we are not closer as a group.

NOW

PETER. It's impossible to know if you're going to get on with people until you actually live with them.

MARTINE. At first I thought people were expecting things from me, but I didn't know what. I was anxious about it. It was my first experience of group living. You only realize how difficult it is to live with people by living with them. Being surrounded by people all the time is sometimes too much.

When Tina and her daughter, Lea, moved in, it was like fresh air to me. I can speak French with Tina, and it is sometimes an extreme relief for me because I can't always make myself clear in English.

TINA. We don't discuss often enough how we all want to live here. I can talk privately to people, but I don't find I can really be myself when we're all in a group together. The group is too skeptical about talking about their deep feelings openly; there isn't enough intimacy among us.

PETER. There are counterpressures to do with living in a group. You're expected to spend time with other people because that's the idea. On the other hand, if I'm going to do work of my own, I have to be alone to do it. Partly as a consequence or living here with this group of people, I have produced far more drawings and paintings than at any other time in my life. The problems and pressures of living here, paradoxically, helped me to get in touch with a seam of personal expressive imagery that was quite new and exciting.

TINA. I'm definitely happier living here in this commune than I'd been in the last two or three years. In a way I feel more independent—free from the burden of having to consider another person's wishes all the time. Since I've been here I've become more positive, more self-confident—in a way, I like myself more. At the beginning I used to feel quite lonely and often resented being here. Now my main interest doesn't lie in the house so I can take people as they are and don't expect more than they can give.

CHRISTINE. I learned what it must be like to be a full-time wife and mother because I was available to do lots of jobs and I spent a lot of time with the kids, but after a while I began to feel resentful. It seemed the women were doing more. It wasn't as if we were wives and being kept. We were still responsible for paying our share of the household expenses. Because of wanting to be equal we were also knocking in nails and fetching wood and fixing windows and decorating and looking after the children, and somehow the balance went wrong. That was the time I began to be angry with Peter, because our idea, when we came here, was to gradually reduce outside work and build a project together. At this time he took his summer holiday off in America—which he had the right to do—but he'd never explained that his idea had changed and the commune wasn't what he'd hoped for, that he wasn't going to give up work, that he was taking his energies away. We've had a lot of nice occasions—picnics, parties, Christmases—but in an ordinary day-to-day way we've failed to work on projects together. Perhaps it's too much to expect.

TINA. There's a very mature attitude to money and chores in this house. No one squabbles about petty things and I like that.

MARTINE. We all take it in turns to cook and clean, and that works well. I now do my share and don't feel guilty about the rest. I am not so concerned about other people's approval now.

CHRISTINE. There haven't been any major crises over money. Occasionally there's been a minor grumble that the household has spent too much. But on the whole it works well—we share all the expenses, even the mortgage, but we have separate money for holidays and all personal expenses.

MARTINE. I think I have grown up quite a lot by living here. I have learned how not to be so self-destructive and how to express my feelings in a more positive way. Anger was something I was unable to express except by getting upset and crying for long periods of time.

PETER. Sometimes I feel disappointed that there aren't more people I could be intellectually close to. I enjoy purposeful conversation but I have no gift for small talk, and this can be a real obstacle in the initial stages of meeting people. Being sociable just for the sake of it rarely attracts me. I am also a bit of a miser and puritan about words. I love to hoard them and usually keep them to myself and a few close friends. These characteristics have generally been seen as negative by other people here.

IAN. At Easter I went to a conference at Lauriston Hall and it clarified my feelings about communes. And most important, I fell in love. That's given me a sense of direction—I hope to go and live with Louis in a commune.

The lifestyle here is all wrong for me. This place is more concerned with aesthetic surroundings than the quality of relationships and, from what I see of Louis, his is totally the other way round. His commune is squatting in a building in London. It's a squalid and chaotic place with one cold water tap and one toilet, for about fifteen people, but it's all right—I like being there. People there are concerned about what's happening to each other and, perhaps most important of all, the majority of the people there are gay, which makes a totally different atmosphere, one which I haven't experienced before but one which I found most comfortable.

MARTINE. We don't do much together at all; most of the time people disappear in the earliest part of the evening and reappear later on. As most of us are out all day, we don't see much of each other. I regret that. We occasionally talk by the fire or watch television; otherwise we have individualistic occupations. I suppose there is no real motivation or drive for us to be together. I often have the feeling that when one of us leaves the group for good there is no feeling of loss, not much regret.

PETER. If each individual's experience were analyzed, you might find that everyone had gone through the process of being reborn; and birth is a painful process—I feel that I've illustrated that in my work. For most of us, a period of withdrawal, often accompanied by depression, has been necessary; and this state has been supported by the communal situation—the household has gone on.

The continual struggle to free ourselves from internalized parents—which I take to be a part of all our experience—seems to become even more stressful and complex in the communal group. So many potential parental and sibling relationships.

MARTINE. I like Fiona and can be close to her. As far as Christine is concerned, it is a very sore point; there is some barrier, a kind of blockage between us which I haven't worked out yet. She is a very good person but it is difficult to get through to her. I can't anyway. I feel threatened by her.

My going to London three days a week was a kind of escape. I had to do something of that sort to be able to get out of the tangle. Now I feel much better and stronger. I don't think I could go back to full time in Ramsgate.

PETER.   I remember a time when I felt it would be a good thing for Maureen to move out because her fluctuations of feelings towards living in a group were an unfair pressure on everyone else.

MAUREEN.   I was always searching for a different place to live but needed money and confidence. I did not want to pressurize anyone else with my emotions and antifeelings. Also, basically I liked several people in the commune who I felt I got on well with and who Reuben liked too. I wanted to live not too far away so no links would be severed irrevocably.

I find it a great relief having moved away—now I'm living with a boyfriend, John; and Reuben. I don't feel I have to divide my energy into eight little parts, which is what I felt before. Now I can settle something with one person rather than having to discuss it with seven others.

I felt my thoughts and actions were in a whirl of confusion the more people that I found around me. I hate messy thoughts. Now I think more clearly. In fact, I wish there were enough islands so everybody could have their own, and little Japanese bridges built across from one to the other for communicating occasionally. Nice to feel the edge or limits of one's physical territory; it eases the mind, too, as we do not have to think beyond these bounds if we don't have the energy to do so.

CHILDREN

PETER. It is a sadness to me that Reuben isn't still living here all the time, I like the idea of his growing up in a mixed household with more than the usual range of personalities, options and interests to take up. Nowadays I don't see enough of him, but I've found it very satisfying that when Reuben comes here I feel very close to him and I don't feel any conflict, which I sometimes used to feel when Maureen was here, too. When we were living as a couple we had stepped out of standard husband-wife roles quite a bit. I did quite a lot of child-care and housework, and Maureen often went out in the evenings.

MAUREEN. I went out to evening classes, also to work at the library, not to gallivant. I invited my friends home at weekends only. I was doing three jobs at once then. Peter cooked and washed up, never cleaned the house.

CHRISTINE. We have had some very good times with the children, and lots of arguments, too, about how they should be treated. There's been a fair amount of negative attitudes toward them—some people just weren't prepared for the demands they made. There was another eight-year-old living with us and he caused quite a few arguments. But I like stormy, passionate kids—it's a sort of honesty I suppose, a directness. I gave up my job, which was teaching disturbed kids in Islington, to move down to Ramsgate and the commune; and when I gave up the local job, I thought, Now I haven't got work to think of, now it will really begin to happen. I'll be able to give all my energy to the commune—perhaps we'll start a free school!

FIONA. I very much like my daughter, Tanya, having lots of people to relate to, rather than just me. And Tanya had a brother-sister relationship with Reuben—they were very attached. The men in the house had no close relationship with her but at least there were men around her. She did not need a substitute father. She sees her own father often and the three of us are close. My bitterness is gone.

MARTINE. I find the men aren't involved enough with the children; they hardly ever cuddle Lea or play with her, for instance. It is a great shame for her. Although I have decided not to have any children myself, I enjoy them very much and like being with them.

TINA. It's relatively easier living in a commune with Lea, who is three, because there are people to share her with me, than it is living with just one other person who is out to work all day. But my criticism of this place is that the men aren't really interested in the children and Lea has no father-figure. The women are all very good with her, but not the men, so this is my main worry. The men are nice to her when necessary, but they never take her on their laps or take her out for a walk or play with her. But on the other hand, if I want to go out to classes or anywhere, there's always someone to look after her, even for a weekend. She's very happy here without me. Whereas when I lived in France with my boyfriend I could never do that—I had no one to leave her with and I could never go out with my boyfriend and our relationship went very stale. It wasn't enriching in any way— it was always going round in circles in our own problems.

MAUREEN. Communes, I think, are great havens for lone mothers and children, as long as they contain men who can take on the father role. The commune has been a great stabilizing influence in Reuben's life, mainly because his father is there and there are other people he has known for four years. He enjoys his weekends and holidays there and yet is glad to come back to his own room here. John and Reuben get on very well.

SEX AND LOVE

PETER. My main feeling, looking back on the period of jealousy and entanglement with Christine and Martine, seems relief that it's not still going on. That Martine seems happier and that I am happier, and I think Christine is. I think there was an element there of acting in accordance with a theory as well as responding to feelings, the theory being that it ought to be possible to have shared sexual relationships and that love was not quantifiable.

CHRISTINE. I had thought that sharing warmth and physical affection and loving would make us happier. But there was as much pain and unhappiness as good times. At first it seemed that it could get better but the tension and negatives increased.

PETER. I like to think that the failure of the situation to continue had to do with the specifics of the people, rather than with its being just not possible for a mixed sexual relationship to succeed over a long period of time. I was very jealous and didn't manage it well. I didn't anticipate the intensity of the feelings I would have that led on to me being depressed.

MAUREEN. The only cure for jealousy is to get away physically from the source; no amount of mental juggling alters the situation.

PETER. Looking back, it seemed my depressed feelings would begin with me feeling jealous and then mushroom into all sorts of other feelings, which would end with me feeling despair about myself, which I would gradually come out of via drawing.

I had produced very little art before moving here, so I must feel the communal situation has been good for me in that respect.

CHRISTINE. I think it was only halfway through Peter's relationship with Martine that I began to understand what Maureen must have felt when I came on the scene. I think I simply hadn't understood before this what jealousy was like. I wrote something to that effect and showed it to everyone. Some discussion did come out of that, I remember. And yet, I feel I've never been really tested as far as jealousy is concerned, in a whole way.

I was sleeping with Ian during some of the time Peter was sleeping with Martine. I liked him at first because he was like my brother! The men in this house have never really been close to each other as far as I know.

MARTINE. We used to share our relationships, but there was a lot of sexual jealousy between us. Not only between the women, but also, very much, between the men; they didn't like each other very much and were incompatible.

I was, emotionally, very involved with Peter and liked Patrick quite a lot. I used to have sexual friendships with both of them; we also used to sleep by three. And Fiona and I slept together.

CHRISTINE. I haven't been close to Fiona. From time to time I've been close to Tina. There was a time when I thought I could be close to Martine, but it just got too much and I had to put up a barrier—it's too dangerous. I mean, my anger boils and bubbles up. It's been exploded so many times, and it's this awful vicious circle of me being angry, Martine being in tears for days and me feeling guilty.

MARTINE. I don't find it easy to cope emotionally in a situation including too many involvements, but I like the idea and I am learning.

I can myself feel quite monogamous when I am in love with someone, but I think I have to work at it and keep experimenting.

CHRISTINE. The relationship between Peter and myself has, most of the time, been good, but there have been periods when it's dipped quite a bit. One of the contributing factors, which made me feel bad, was what I was seeing as other people's passivity—Ian and Martine's—and recognizing that I had played a part in encouraging that passivity by being overhelpful. Because of the way I was, at one bad period I experienced one member as a parasite. I couldn't bear to say that and then I saw that it didn't have to be —I could stop feeding. That discovery was very liberating, and yet when I did that I became haunted. There was always this figure in my head—wanting—it was awful!

PETER. Meeting Christine opened me up sexually. I value having gone through the experimental sexual periods of this group, although at times it was extremely difficult and rarely joyful. There was a lot of uncertainty about people's motives. I have met contradictions in myself while living here. My theoretical platform would still be for openness sexually, but I have learnt that my actual capacity to cope with it is much more limited than I thought.

CHRISTINE. Ths business of sharing—yes, it becomes a bit of a business. The joy and fun were gone. It was generating so much unhappiness. There seemed no peace or pleasure. Also, there were a lot of practical things—I'd get myself into a role of doing too much, of doing more than my share, and it took me a long time to learn not to do things like other people's share of the housework.

PETER. In the first years I would often have difficulty in being satisfactorily on my own because of being preoccupied about what was going on elsewhere in the house.

Having a primary emotional attachment to somebody, while being aware that they were sleeping with someone else, was a situation that didn't lead to settled feelings. That's an understatement! It is impossible not to have some expectations towards one another; these just grow up implicitly.

CHRISTINE. Till that time I had always been in this room with Peter. I moved downstairs—I needed a space, a physical space for me. I moved into the cellar, which was in a dreadful state; I had to scrape off the walls and make this place habitable, but it was very therapeutic for me. There was a bad tangle. Peter had been sleeping with Martine; Maureen was still in the house and there was a sort of relationship going on between her and Peter. I'd always known this and I hadn't expected this to be different—they'd had years together and Reuben was between them.

But Martine expected too much. Peter and I spent a lot of time worrying about Martine, always talking about her, neglecting ourselves. There were a lot of rows and at one time I experienced myself as being an awful person. I had thought that whatever negative things happened in a commune, never mind, it would be a good learning situation. Then I realized I was learning all bad things and it seemed very destructive. I felt utterly worthless. Then, finally, I realized that that was necessary. If you're learning about yourself then the last things you want to find out are the bad things. Yet that's important too—they help to free you.

PETER. It used to be one of the problematic times, the approach to bedtime, when in this household there were a number of potential partnerships going on. It was an awkward time with a lot of hovering about. It seemed that some people covertly made the decisions and others just let things happen to them. This dichotomy in styles of thinking and acting has recurred in other areas of our life together.

MAUREEN. Perhaps I joined in for the wrong reasons. I was living with my ex-husband and the girlfriend who, in a sense, broke up the marriage. I could accept it intellectually but never emotionally. So whenever there was any conflict between Christine and me, it went really bitter. Once I physically attacked her in front of everyone. I was desperate. After it everyone was silent; they all tried to pretend it hadn't happened. Looking back on it, it would have been much better if we'd all talked about it instead of burying it all in silence.

CHRISTINE. We *did* talk about it.

MAUREEN. I did not want to talk about it, yet in a way I was very glad it happened. It sorted out for me what I really had to do— to go.

Now I feel so ashamed about that part of my life. I seemed to go around crazily looking for reassurance and love. It was valuable in the sense that I learned what can soon make a person neurotic.

PETER. I remember Maureen saying once (but only once!) that she was grateful to me for the situation I had created by my relationship with Christine because she had had so many friends and sexual experiences during that time, through which she'd learnt a lot.

MAUREEN. We were both virgins. After two or three years Peter said, "Well, this isn't very much fun, is it? Shouldn't it be more exciting than this?" Somehow I thought it was the man who had to teach the woman. I think we were more like brother and sister, but I didn't know this till I'd had some affairs and thought, Well, I'd better start exploring myself and start exploring other people's bodies too. So I did, and then I found I was having quite a good time. I started really enjoying it. I was discovering things about myself and about sex.

PETER. The experience of taking acid was very important to me. The first time was at Christmas, just after we moved in. Martine, Christine and I took it and we went through a whole repertoire of emotional experiences individually.

At this very early period in the commune it brought us very close together, and would usually end with us sleeping together. I remember some very beautiful evenings with perhaps six of us taking acid and a long night in the room downstairs. I do feel some regret that that no longer happens. That to some extent the risks and excitement have gone.

MARTINE. I am still very fond of Peter and I still wish we could sleep together, but we don't and I accept it.

MAUREEN. I think I could have accepted the commune situation if there had been enough attractive men to go round, but the ratio of women to men that were interested in women was low. I really like the one man–one woman situation better, although I do a lot more domestic work and there is a danger of falling into the typical male-female roles, which never happened in the commune.

TINA. I want to live in a situation where I have the freedom to be myself all the time without rejection. I need strong relationships and here, I feel, these are avoided. There is something empty. If we could just talk to each other more . . . if we could just say things.

I've been brought up to be free to touch people and show affection, but here there is a feeling of oh, what's she after, does she want to go to bed with me? I feel if we acted more on impulse, more would happen. Here every possibility has to be weighed and the consequences worked out, rather than doing it and seeing what happens. I can only get really close to people if I can be intense with them. If I can't, then there's no bond.

MAUREEN. I couldn't get full sexual enjoyment in the commune.

Perhaps I was too neurotic about people listening, too tense in case my friends were not happy in the house where my ex-husband lived. Men from outside often thought women in communes had loose morals, and there was the fear of being used. I used to feel for the other girls in the house as regards this.

I have still to find a peaceful place with plenty of sky and water and few inhabitants, where one can create with few interruptions. We are saving hard for this. John is becoming less urbanized.

FIONA. I got into quite a close couple relationship with Patrick, which neither of us had planned. By the time I arrived some of the more wild sexual experiments had finished. One of the big mattresses had been moved out of Peter's room and, although we talked of putting it back, it didn't happen. I moved too cautiously—I felt I wanted some liberating sexual experiences. It turned out, though, that sufficient closeness did not develop to rid me of my fears about, for example, group encounters. Three of us slept together occasionally, but this couldn't have become regular practice for me.

CHRISTINE. There are very few people I could break down in front of—Peter, Ian and Tina. Anger comes easily to me but in recent times I've learnt to actively avoid conflict. I imagined everyone would be open—open up to each other—but that hasn't happened all that much and I guess I've accepted that now.

I know I don't want to be married. I feel things will change in my life. I haven't got a particular definite way of life I want.

IAN. Men generally don't expect warm, supportive relationships from men, and this is what I want—warmth from other guys. And that is the tone of the London commune where Louis lives.

It's very good for me to be in a situation where I know being gay is totally approved of. I'm still paranoid in the straight world that someone's going to say, "Get away from that pervert."

FIONA. I still want a close central sexual relationship, but perhaps not one where every waking moment I was quite so closely involved. Perhaps I would rather have my practical domestic environment separate—to live in a different house from my lover, so that it would be purely a matter of choice when we came together. If you live together it inevitably becomes heavy and over-whelming.

MARTINE. I know that I dread the idea of marriage, which traps you in a closed situation. I want to feel free for moving and changing when I need to. I also like my emotional bonds to be secret—they don't have to be known by everybody.

MAUREEN. I think now sex is paramount—it affects my whole next day. It's got to be good—my functioning becomes slower, my whole look at life becomes grayer if I don't have a good sex life. And when I was here that was my main problem—I wasn't having a good sex life.

POLITICS

PETER. I sometimes think that the difference between living this way and living how most other people do is easy to take for granted. It's to do with interpersonal relations; the business of living closely with six or seven other people, and that as a con-tinuing experience, would mark living in a commune as very dif-ferent from living with one other person.

This area of Kent is "depressed"—young people move away. The social ambience is stuffily conservative.

MAUREEN. There seemed to be an anarchic taboo in the early years about organizing chores. I remember I could not join in anything so unorganised; otherwise I would have done my share.

CHRISTINE. I want the chores to be done efficiently so there is time for other things. I wanted us to get together, to put our energies together to do creative things as a commune. Then I realized that other people had different ideas. Some people just wanted a nice place to be with other people—warmth. Perhaps there was a lack in me that I couldn't take people's warmth—I wanted to do things, practical things. Things to do with children—run some kind of play school, start a free school. But I had to realize that people had very different ideas about what a commune should be. I had to realize that my anger was due to my own dissatisfaction, and not because people were bad.

PETER. There have been a few communal projects and events here. Once we had a communal painting session, and we all joined in on painting a big board in a completely free way. I would like to have built on the experience of that, to involve the group in a more prestructured situation, in producing coherent results. But other people were dubious about it. Another time we used the playroom to play together—the project was playing—and we did all the nursery kinds of things, like dressing up.

MAUREEN. There were good things. One of the main things was how tolerant people were. People let each other be—there wasn't nasty gossip behind each other's backs. The other thing was the economical way it was run—there was a commitment to simplicity and lack of greed, which I liked. Also they'd harbor people for a short time, not run them down for not working. And then, a great acceptance for children.

THE FUTURE

PETER. I have thought about living alone with Christine. Currently she and I don't spend a lot of time together because of our work schedules—I work during the day and she is often out in the evening, and often going to London for odd days.

CHRISTINE. Now I move in and out of this house more freely than I did in the first two years when I had a strong feeling about the "it" of this place. Now I think of it as simply the place where I live, while in the beginning I thought that a commune was about giving up individual aims and working collectively.

I have felt like leaving at times but my relationship with Peter is important to me, and also I've put a lot of energy into this place and I don't feel like moving down the road and paying six pounds a week again.

Perhaps my security is my work again—I teach remedial students and it's a very delicate relationship, not one I can easily walk out on.

TINA.   I have always led a rather restless sort of life, full of changes. Now I have Lea I feel I should provide her with something stable. She needs a father-figure to relate to, preferably someone I could be close to as well.

MARTINE.   I like Ramsgate as a place and I love the sea. I have strong feelings of "belonging" to the commune but somehow I feel it is not right for me. I have been here for four years now. I feel it is coming to an end. I am restless with my life anyway, I need changes. I never plan long in advance. I know when the good opportunity is here and I grab it.

FIONA.   Ramsgate was liberating because here I escaped from being a wife. But in the end I had a feeling of dissatisfaction. I couldn't get close enough to all the people and I still haven't worked out if it was the particular way our personalities went together or unrealistic expectations. The only person I got as close to as I wanted was Tina.

As far as organizing the place went, it ran well—it was fine. It was a supportive environment. The sharing of financial and practical burdens is a great advance over the nuclear family setup. It released energy for other activities. For me it also eliminated friction and oppressiveness from my couple relationship.

My feeling of responsibility for Tanya began to weigh heavier. I decided she needed permanence but I didn't want to settle in Ramsgate for the rest of her school life. So we are moving to London, to another communal situation of course; I feel committed to this way of life.

I started a play group but the response was terribly disappointing. Ramsgate was too dead, too respectable; we had almost no friends. It didn't open up communication with the town, which is what we had hoped for. I didn't know how to mobilize outside support, although I knew how to run the play group itself. I was working on this completely on my own within the commune. The others were passively approving but not actively interested. It's a pity; this was a potential community project that didn't get off the ground and we didn't have any others.

MAUREEN. Living with John is very good. I feel progress in all directions—my work and communicating. There are no doors to close.

I work at home, making jewelry mainly in silver, selling enough to live on. John and I keep finances on an equal basis. I feel we have a good relationship with the commune now. Reuben goes to stay every fortnight and half the holidays in Ramsgate. They are our friends.

Without the umbrella of the commune I would not have had the financial ease and friendly support to get my craft off the ground. It was a slow, arduous slog at which I spent many hours per day, with the knowledge my evening meal was cooked and Reuben playing happily somewhere in the house. This I was, and am now, very grateful for.

CHRISTINE. I had lived on my own before this and I liked that, so when I got my own room again I began to get my self-confidence back and to feel I could be on my own. But I do feel disappointed that we haven't got a communal thing going.

Sometimes I've felt I'd like to live with just Peter. Sometimes I've felt I'd like to live on my own. I think I'm very work-oriented—I like working. This business of living with other people, it leaves everything open to examination. Every attitude is open to question; it's very exhausting. I thrive on purposeful activity—thinking or discussing or dancing—but meandering, sitting about, I'm impatient. I've had to go away and focus my energies on what I want to do. Some people in this house think that spontaneity is the way things happen, and other people think you have to decide what you want and make it happen. There was a lot of argument about spontaneity versus planning.

FIONA. Looking back, I enjoyed things like cooking and organizing the household shopping and equipment with other people, trying to make the household run smoothly without having sole responsibility and worry.

Playing the piano was a great release for me. I would have liked to involve the others in this pleasure. It didn't often happen —in the sense of expressing ourselves together; everyone was busy with other things. I did help Martine and Tina to start learning the piano.

Group things didn't happen often enough for me. It was really a group of individuals living together rather than trying to create one whole.

In spite of the obvious difficulties at Ramsgate, there was so much to be learned about communal living from their conflicts and their successes.

One positive thing I noticed immediately was how well and easily the housekeeping and finances worked. Nobody drowned in domesticity. It was cheap to live there and yet everybody had a light, spacious room, and the food was terrific (perhaps Martine's being French was an influence on that!).

It is a struggle living in a commune. This was true of both Leeds and Brighton. A different kind of struggle from that of living within an ordinary family. I wish I had done it at some time in my life—perhaps I might still. After all, there's no age limit. To relate to several people over such domestic things as sugar and at the same time not hide depression, misery and anger seems an enormous challenge.

Why aren't I doing it right now? It doesn't seem to be the moment; I'm into a private relationship. (As Jem said about his teacher, "She's into Jesus," so I might say, "I'm into Dan.") But I don't really expect relationships to last forever and next time round I might do it differently.

I can think of very few people I would care to share a house with—I think Carola being family makes a difference.

10. LIVING WITH YOUR SISTER: CAROLA, NICKY, IAN . . . AND ROGER

' *Carola, Nicky and Ian live in an early-Victorian semi-detached villa with an enormous garden where they grow vegetables.*

Carola lives upstairs with her son, Joshua, who is nine. Nicky and Ian live downstairs with their adopted son and daughter, Caspar, three, and Rosie, ten months.

Their setup is special because Carola and Nicky are sisters. They both got married and needed somewhere to live in London around the same time, so they decided to share a house and a mortgage, and ended up sharing quite a lot more.

After a while, Adam (who was married to Carola) left, leaving Carola to look after Josh. Carola (who had trained as a designer), in order to support them both and to get herself out of a depression, started a shop in Portobello Road with a friend, selling, among other things, children's clothes.

In the meantime, Nicky and Ian had been waiting to adopt, and finally Caspar arrived, and then Rosie. So Nicky left work [she was a photographic studio assistant] and stayed at home bringing up her babies—but also being a second mother to Josh when Carola was at work. Ian is a freelance photographer who teaches at the Central College of Art, in London. He seems to take being a second dad to Josh and supportive male to Carola in his stride.

It seems almost Victorian to come to a house where two sisters are sharing so much, including pleasure in each other's company. The first time I went there, Carola cooked lunch upstairs, where Nicky and Caspar ate with us. Next time, Nicky cooked downstairs and Carola made the dessert and brought it down.

Since I began writing this, Roger, an architect, who is Carola's boyfriend, has moved in, and Roger's little son, Gus, who is Caspar's age, comes for weekends often. If it isn't pouring with rain —and sometimes when it is—summer or winter, they all go out on Ian's boat up the canal. At the end Roger, as the newcomer, says what he thinks about it all.

They all pay rent, which pays the mortgage. They divide up the local taxes, gas and electricity bills. On the whole, the bills are split down the middle. They share a washing machine and other bits of equipment. Ian does the garden—he's growing vegetables now. **99**

NOW

NICKY.   Almost as soon as I was old enough I moved into a flat of my own and got a job. I couldn't wait to leave school—what I always wanted was to go out and leave home and earn my own living. Now I tremendously enjoy my domestic life and I feel slightly bitter with women's lib, who make you feel you shouldn't enjoy it.

CAROLA. I would always want to work at something. When I was solely a housewife, I did find it restricting. So in a way the shop is a creation—people can see it and they come and use it. I'm definitely not solely domestic. I'd been in a dreadful troughlike depression and the shop got me out of that.

NICKY. I don't feel like a cabbage. I spend quite a lot of time cooking—we like food. I take the children out a lot and I make all Caspar's and Rosie's clothes, and I used to make all Ian's shirts and trousers and all my own clothes.

CAROLA. We don't particularly share our social life. When I was first on my own I did try to invite people round for dinner, but in the end I just didn't have the time or the energy. And I hated the whole situation and thought people were coming thinking, "Poor Carola, she's on her own," so I gave up.

IAN. I like being the dominant male in the house—I've been it for so many years. I like doing things around the house. If I had a private income and didn't have to work, I'd be quite happy just to putter about, to run a community or something. I love working with my hands—I'd much rather do things with my hands than with my brain.

NICKY. When I drive through the suburbs and see all these little units with their separate cars and gardens, I get an awful feeling of doom and boredom. Their lives look so ordered and so alike. I know I couldn't bear it. I need outside stimulus, I couldn't stand a sterile, turned-in family life. Also, on the practical side, it means Ian and I can have time to ourselves. Carola can take over and the children are equally happy up there. We can always go out at night. If we are all going out, we can share the cost of a baby-sitter.

IAN. We have the boat on the canal at Uxbridge, and that's like a movable country cottage to get away to.

NICKY. This weekend we all went out on the boat: Joshua and his friend, Carola and Roger and Roger's little boy, and Ian and me and the babies. And it was chaotic with all the children, but really great fun—more fun than if we'd been on our own.

IAN.   I never feel alone in the house. I'm thinking of my sister and brother-in-law who live in a flat and don't know anybody around them, and I just get the impression they're terribly lonely there. It's never lonely here—you just wander up and down when you want to; though territories are very well established and we do have our privacy—we can close the door between us.

NICKY.   Once Carola started the shop she became much more independent. It seems to suit her, being a working woman.

IAN.   I can think of very few people I would care to share a house with—I think Carola being family makes a difference.

CHILDREN

CAROLA.   When my husband left, I was a freelance designer, but it was difficult. I couldn't work in the day because Josh was always around me, so I had to work in the evenings.

It was badly paid and we lived very close to the borderline. Josh went to a nursery school and nearly everything I earned went on paying for that. So I got together with a friend and we started the shop. For a long time we could only make a little money, and it was then I realized how bitterly I resented having no money and that I wanted a lot more. I tried Social Security but the whole thing seemed so difficult I couldn't go through with it. Now, finally, I'm in a position where I can pay the gas bill, but I'd like to be able to spend money without so much anxiety. All the money I earn is strictly allocated—luxuries don't figure, but perhaps they don't for most people.

Joshua has spent almost as much time downstairs with Nicky and Ian as upstairs with me. As Adam left when he was tiny, he got very fond of Ian. I was then working till six every evening and every other Saturday, and Nicky and Ian had Josh.

Then, two years ago, Nicky and Ian adopted Caspar, who Josh regards really as a brother, so in a sense Josh's family became me, Nicky, Ian and Caspar. Then, a month ago, Ian and Nicky got Rosie.

NICKY. Josh is devoted to Ian—he does all the masculine things with him. Carola and I are both so wet. Caspar adores Josh; as soon as he hears him come back from school, he calls to him.

IAN. I don't feel under pressure to be responsible for Joshua. When I've got time I play with him, but when I haven't I can tell him. I'm very fond of him.

CAROLA. Ian's very soft and also does lots of things Josh can join in, like run a boat, or a steam engine, go fishing.

IAN. At the weekends we often go away in the boat and then I have lots of time for the kids—I just relax and enjoy them.

NICKY. Then, of course, there's Caspar. He adores Carola; she is his second mother and he's as happy upstairs with her as downstairs with me.

CAROLA. I quite often look after Caspar in the evenings, or occasionally at a weekend. I love Caspar and so does Josh. He's no bother or strain to have about.

NICKY. I think you've got to accept that once you've got children your life is going to change. But you needn't become a drudge, it needn't become boring. I get impatient with people who treat their children as a nuisance. I suppose I feel it especially as I wasn't able to have children, as I had cancer. And it took us six years to adopt Caspar.

CAROLA. Joshua would have been happier if he'd had a brother or a sister—it hasn't been easy for him being an only child. Without Ian and Nicky, I don't know how I would have managed.

SEX AND LOVE

CAROLA.   After I'd split with Adam I was very wary about making permanent relationships. Also, I seemed to meet mostly men who were married, and it just didn't work out. And Joshua didn't like me going out. He was upset by meeting lots of different people and would say things like, "Are you going to stay the night?" which was embarrassing. Sometimes he'd say, "Why don't you marry my Mommy?" I found all this very hard and I felt continually guilty. I'd work all day and in the evenings Joshua and I would stay in together. If we went out, it was to see my parents, or with Nicky and Ian on their boat. We had a cosy little setup; it was undemanding—we'd go to the pictures or watch television.

If I had a boyfriend, he'd only arrive late at night or I'd go out to meet him and rush home. But that would be at the most twice a week; otherwise Josh would be upset at my not being there. My life was, in a way, bound by his demands. Poor little boy— I used to hate my parents' going out. At the same time, I did feel shut in and it was difficult to make relationships.

Once you have children your life has to be centered on the home. Therefore you've got to make a scene there.

I didn't like boyfriends sleeping in the house. I was uneasy about what Josh would feel.

I hated doing social things on my own, like going out to dinner or having people in or going to the theater, and I didn't have anyone to do these things with. I wanted a boyfriend to do all these things with. I didn't particularly mind if he lived down the road— I just wanted someone so I could overcome this awful business of always turning up at places on my own. I felt such an undesirable proposition and I got more and more shut in.

That and the money were the worst things—I was very unhappy. Perhaps what I should really have been worrying about was having a close relationshp with a smashing man, but in fact that seemed to be secondary.

I fell in love with married men and became extremely good at being tactful. It just makes you feel there's nothing to you but a bit of light relief, that nobody is ever going to take you seriously.

I did have a few good friends. I couldn't have gone through it without them. But, most important of all, I had Nicky and Ian.

NICKY. I lived with Ian for two years before we were married. Our mother encouraged us to live with our boyfriends before we got married.

CAROLA. When we were children, Nicky and I hated each other. We just didn't get on at all. As adolescents it was particularly bad.

When Nicky was seventeen she decided she was going to leave home and she did—she's much the more independent of us. I've always been terribly dependent on my parents. As a child I couldn't bear them being out in the evenings, and then when I was grown up, I couldn't bear them being out of London for a weekend or away on their holidays.

NICKY. The way we live was never a cold-blooded decision, it just grew up gradually.

I don't feel jealous about sharing Ian because if he has to choose between us and upstairs, we come first.

IAN. I'm useful in a very practical sense, but I leave the emotional side to Nicky and Carola.

CAROLA. It might have been hard for Nicky over the last five or six years. Josh and I were alone upstairs and we relied on Ian for lots of things, like mending the phonograph or being a sort of alternative father for Joshua. It was hard on her having to share her husband in lots of ways.

We are pretty open with each other but we don't actually have rows, except when we're staying with my parents; then we are both feeling uneasy and can be quite aggressive towards each other.

Nicky is a tremendous prop to me. Every night when I come home from work, I spend at least half an hour downstairs talking to her. I go down to see the babies before Ian comes home, and fetch Josh who's usually down there. I find now I really need to do it after a day at work.

NICKY. I don't really need support from Carola because I've got

Ian, but if I quarrel with Ian I go upstairs to Carola for commiseration.

CAROLA. I don't think we've suffered with jealousy between us. Nicky is sensitive and sensible and knows that it was good for Josh having a close relationship with Ian. Also, Ian loves children. Caspar hasn't pushed Josh out as he's six years younger—it's really been like a younger brother coming along.

NICKY. Sometimes, if Ian and I are disagreeing about something and Carola turns up, we get her to arbitrate. We used to have endless screaming rows but now we only have arguments.

CAROLA. I do feel guilty sometimes. They've been tremendously supportive to me all the time, picking up the pieces when I've had a broken love affair and I've got the rough end of the stick. Ian and Nicky have fed me in more ways than one—they've been my absolute prop. I value my relationship with Nicky more than anything else.

When Roger moved in they were very encouraging. "Yes, you must do it," they said; "it will be good for Joshua. Why not try it?"

IAN. When Roger first moved in I felt very jealous and threatened. When Carola was living here with Adam it was dreadful—we couldn't agree about anything. Then he went and for the next six years I managed everything until a couple of months ago, when Roger moved in with Carola. So far he's left me to get on with running things and it's all going smoothly.

CAROLA. It's a fear—marriage was somehow a trap and I was in a humiliating position. Now, every time Roger moves something in, I wonder, Is it going to go or is it going to stay? I don't want any more responsibility—nor do I want to be under obligation. I still think of him as a visitor in the house; I still feel I'm the one that should say where a chair goes.

When I feel insecure about Roger, I see myself as a useful scene—I've got a house, a car, a place where he can bring his child at weekends.

NICKY. I find it very hard to tell Carola if I'm irritated about something. On the whole, we can tell if the other is in a bad mood, then we can retreat into our own private place.

When Adam was living here there was an amazing amount of tension. Since their marriage broke up, there have been no major difficulties and very few disagreements.

IAN. It seems a very tame situation—it really works so easily.

CAROLA. I think that for me, Nicky and Ian have become the stability in my life. I need them. I can't imagine anybody else living there, I wouldn't want anybody else living there. There is a constant to-ing and fro-ing between us. Although there is a door that shuts us off, it is always open.

WHERE TO?

IAN. Sometimes I feel very complacent about my lfe—it seems incredibly good. There's never any shortage of things to do here. There's the garden, the vegetable garden, the compost, the house to keep together, toys to mend for the children. I like doing things all the time. I like variety. I see no reason why it shouldn't go on growing and changing in this house.

CAROLA. Ian and Roger get on well, and now there is another male in the house, it's lifted the pressure off Ian. I think in a way he felt responsible for me and Josh.

I'd definitely like more weekends to ourselves—one doesn't know how long relationships are going to last, after all. Roger and I have very little time to ourselves.

ROGER'S VIEW

ROGER. Carola hadn't had anyone living with her for seven years. Nicky and Ian were her family. I had to tread very gently, but the situation seemed full of potential—there was room for something else to come into it.

My most difficult part was how carefully I had to move. I started with absolutely no status; I was just the "boyfriend." Although in my life I'm not concerned with permanence, I am concerned with contributing to a situation. Every moment matters —you can't afford to waste your life.

The separation between upstairs and downstairs has in some ways increased and in others decreased. There is a more formal arrangement.

Before I was there I think there was very little life going on upstairs; now there is an equal balance of life in both places. I think it gives Carola more of a sense of her own being. So the relationships can be fuller ones now the dependence has lessened.

The trivia of life, such as untidiness and meal times, are so important, and we had great difficulty sorting all this out.

I moved in three weeks after meeting Carola, with a couple of shirts. I brought very little because although I like possessions, I don't really have an attachment to them—they belong to a time in my life rather than to myself. It was quite a step when I went from having half a drawer in Carola's chest of drawers to the time when I actually got half of a wardrobe to myself.

I was aware that in Carola's house life had stood still since Adam left. Some objects are long-term and one doesn't expect them to change, like sofas and chairs. But an article cut out of a newspaper and pinned on the wall is transient. Yet there was a whole collection of that kind of thing which had remained static. It was as if the upstairs half of the house had been used as a hotel for Carola and Josh—it had that quality of seven years ago. I started with the bathroom when I arrived. It was orange, with peeling wallpaper. The first thing I did was change the bath taps.

I come from the post–nineteen sixty-eight generation and I've always felt part of this. Carola is six years older than me and we have very different sets of friends. So we had a serious problem with our close friends. I was, according to my friends, moving from a freak subculture to a straight subculture and they couldn't quite accept that. Now it all seems to matter much less. Although it is important to find social stimulus somewhere.

I left my wife when Gus, my son, was two, and now I suddenly have found myself in a situation where I am dealng with a child of nine. I found it difficult to gain his respect in a way that he would understand. It took me about six months and I felt, finally, that I had won it when I could give Josh a belt without his resenting it.

I found it surprising how easy it became for me to have a relationship with Josh because I was living with him. It's more difficult for me to have a relationship with Gus because of the lack of time for us. I only have him to stay every other weekend.

As far as I'm concerned, the only way of solving it is for more people to grow around each other. I'd like Gus and his mother to live near us and to be part of our scene. I'm unhappy about my situation with Gus—I haven't resolved it at all. I'm seeking to but it's very difficult to have a part-time relationship with a small child.

I came from a secure Jewish suburban family. I think having roots was immensely important to me and I'd like to give Gus some of this tribal feeling, some framework to move against. The beauty, to me, of a community is to have a group of people around who are in strongly caring interwoven relationships of intimacy.

I feel I'm in a situation where I'm on test all the time. But I like it, it's the way I like to live. Just because I'm an outsider I can see the parts of this situation that don't work. There's no way that I can compete on the level of time and blood ties. All I can do is offer something entirely different. And for some strange reason, they're all prepared to view me with an honesty and a freshness, just seeing what I am going to do next. And I hope I can contribute something which has not yet quite pulled the situation together.

It's a turn-on for me—this house, the boat, the children, the whole situation.

In a way I'm the least important person here. My position is the least stable, but, in another way, it's the most conscious. Because I'm not part of the family but I've chosen to be here, it means that I'm the most free—I'm here because I want to be here.

What I feel would be most difficult for me about Carola's situation is that it is so anchored in her childhood, her family, and therefore somehow in the past. So that Roger, entering this stronghold, is in some way bound to be an intruder. All those problems of property and ownership that keep rearing their heads in my life are there. What I really want to be is a gypsy with a big light bright room or two in the middle of the city overlooking a park. And I identify with Roger when he says he is the most free.

The other point he brings up is friends. I want to go on having close friends and yet it's more difficult, living with someone. So much of my emotional energy is directed towards Dan. I used to be a loner and to go about with other loners. Now I'm not a loner, but I still feel determined to go on going off on my own, to stay with my friends.

All the people who live in this house are people who've been through difficult things, who wanted an atmosphere where they could find out who they were and wanted to develop themselves in relation to other people—the sense of extended family really just happened out of the needs of people who were here.

11. ONE HOUSE, THREE WOMEN, FOUR CHILDREN AND THE ARTS: DINAH, ALEX AND SHEILA

Dinah, Alex and Sheila have been living together for about four years. Others have come and gone but the heart of the house is the three women and four children: Emily and Joe, Dinah's twins, aged nine; and Michael and Patrick, aged thirteen and nine, who are Sheila's. Alex has no children but has a peculiar, almost magic, facility for relating to them.

Dinah says most, because I talked to her twice and we knew each other before. Also, her situation has a lot in common with mine. We are the same age, we both own a house "in trust," have children, don't live with husbands and are writers.

Sheila is American. She is a sculptress who upholsters for money. Alex is also American. She is an actress and a therapist who had a lot of trouble with her work permit, so lately she married Steve, now also living in the house.

Dinah's father, who is seventy, lives with them for about six months of the year; the other six he spends with her mother.

A man walks in. A child calls out, "It's George!"

"George who?"

"George archeologist."

Around the kitchen table sit Dinah's father, Sheila, all four children just back from school, and George. Dinah walks back and forth making tea, and crumpets sprinkled with cinnamon and sugar. George talks of his latest dig. The children talk among themselves and then join in the adult conversation about Colette and then Poona, where they're going in India. They're worried about losing their friends, and Emily's music teacher had told her she can't play the viola in India—it's too hot. We wondered which would melt, Emily or her viola.

Dinah is a follower of Bagwan, a great believer in "letting go," giving way to the continual fluctuations in life as opposed to attempting to control everything around you. A deeply anti-repressive philosophy—love, joy, be who you are. Indeed, around the table, although we talked among other things of the arts, I didn't get the feeling anyone was trying to make an impression on anyone else—there we were.

The house belongs to Dinah. Everyone pays a specific amount of rent. There is a communal food budget. On a rota system, each person, including the children, is responsible for shopping, cooking, cleaning and looking after the animals.

Living there at the moment are Dinah and Emily and Joe, Sheila and Michael and Patrick, Alex, John, Steve. **"**

WHERE FROM?

SHEILA. My marriage was very conventional; neither of us slept around, although I always fantasized about it. My husband, Jim, just tried to dominate me all the time. Twice I thought he was going mad he was so heavy.

The first time I started going mad was when I was pregnant with Michael. My husband was nine years older than me—I was twenty-three when I got married. He had had almost no sexual experience and he had a very romantic idea of marriage—cocktails for two in a penthouse. He expected me to be all dressed up when he came home from work, with my hair done and makeup on and the martinis cooling in the refrigerator. I wasn't supposed to be tired, and dinner was supposed to be ready, and it was always supposed to be that way. And if I didn't have black bikini knickers on, he would pout.

I was supposed to be a glamour puss, and if I veered from that he got very upset. But I just wasn't like that. I wanted to wear sandals, with my hair streaming down my face, and he'd get so angry—it didn't suit his fantasy. He hadn't been that way before we were married.

We'd known each other five months. He was such a nice considerate guy. Then suddenly, we're married and I'm pregnant and he'd come home from the university (he was a university professor) and talk about all the beautiful figures all his students had. And here I am getting fatter by the minute and he watching every potato I ate. And he didn't really even want to talk about my pregnancy—it was just a big drag to him. He was always afraid to talk to me. He pretended we didn't have any problems. He'd walk away.

We were living in Puerto Rico with no English-speaking people around. I was so lonely. I fantasized all the time, every single day, all day, till the day Michael was born. And that day we were so happy—he was such a fantastic baby—talking about the future. I had no fantasies that day. And the next day Jim came to the hospital, and when the nurse brought in the food he wouldn't let me eat any potatoes. All he did was talk about how soon I'd get my old figure back. And I just went flying back to my old fantasy world where people had accepted me and loved me the way I was. But Jim was always trying to control me and push me into even looking a different way, and he'd even criticize the things I'd say when we went out. He'd pull me aside and say, "Why did you say that?" in an angry voice.

I took nine years to get out of my marriage because although I knew I'd made a horrendous mistake, I couldn't really face it. I was just too crushed, it broke my heart.

DINAH. Between twelve and seventeen I read nothing but young ladies' magazines, and I got the idea that my destiny was to marry a tall, dark, handsome architect who would look after me; and I would be a good wife and mother and cook apple pie and make lampshades and be around.

Then I married Frank and the twins were born. I had live-in housekeepers because I felt, I've got to write. I've got to have time to myself to write; I shall go mad if I don't. I was manic— I just had to write. If I didn't have the mornings to myself I used to think I was going mad.

I only cared about the amount of solitude I could get. I pussyfooted around my demands on my husband. Even though he was in the house all day, because he was a writer too, it was always me who was expected to be responsible for the children. It hadn't occurred to either of us, way back in the sixties, to work out some reasonable way to share the responsibility for the kids.

We each had to have a room to write in. We each had to have the mornings free and couldn't stand hearing any noise while we were working.

I remember a friend in the women's movement, when I told her this, said, "But your demands are too great, you cannot make these demands!"

I can't make any sense out of my relationship with Frank in a few lines. We got married because our neuroses matched, perhaps, and the marriage was a process of working them out. Later he went along with the idea of living communally, and took his turns cooking and doing the dishes and walking the kids to school, but he was desperately miserable. After two years we separated, not so much because of living with other people. The living with other people had been, for me, the beginning of an attempt to free myself from the marriage.

CHILDREN

SHEILA. I'm delighted about my children having such a close relationship with Dinah's kids. The basement is only two rooms, and yet they have a whole house, a whole world, as their home. They're very happy kids. I have no problems with them.

When I have a man around me, they do enjoy it and try and get some of his attention. I left their father when Patrick was four and Michael was eight; and perhaps it's a little boy's fantasy to possess their mother and suddenly they did—and I was so much happier. I used to wake up with a smile on my face for about six months—it was such a relief not to have that horrible pressure of a bad relationship. I was so much more relaxed and I had more to give to the kids.

DINAH. I've been living with four kids around the house for about four years, and attempting to treat all in the same way. I spent last summer with a friend—she'd been living alone with her two kids and their relationship was so cosy and familial and full of little jokes and stories and teasing. They'd been spending a lot of time on each other, which I haven't been spending on my kids. I've been trying to relate to ten different people all at once, so that I haven't really spent five minutes concentrating on my kids alone for four years.

It had been a chore and a duty and everyone was telling me, "You treat your kids in such a terrible way!" People were saying to me, on the one hand, "You never give your kids any attention," and on the other hand, "For God's sake leave those fucking kids alone and listen to me for a minute. You know, when I come to have coffee with you, all you do is fuss about those bloody kids; why don't you just sit and be there for me." And I just didn't know where I was.

And now I don't want to be there for an anonymous mass of people. I can't bear people coming into the kitchen and just sitting around and expecting me to chat; I don't want to talk to them. I want to have my own place and I want to talk to the people I want to talk to. And I want to be with my kids, and I want to concentrate on them, and I want to develop a real proper relationship with them. I want to talk to them, and I want to look at them and listen to them. I don't want to spend my energy on other kids because I don't have that amount of energy.

ALEX. I've got a fantastic amount out of living with the four children in this house. It's been a stunning insight into how people are with their children and how conditioned their behavior is by their own upbringing—and also that if you want to change, with awareness you can change anything.

Dinah struck me as someone who had never had any experience other than deprivation, and she was depriving her own children, but she didn't know what she was depriving them of. And to see how in the last year or two her children have developed, and the warmth and love that is between them now—that's given me the courage to think that I possibly might have a child of my own and that one doesn't have to relate to one's children in terms of the jungle of one's own childhood.

DINAH. Last year I took Emily skiing, and this was special because it was just us two, so it was a magic time. But I find it difficult to sort out this time thing. I can stay upstairs talking or reading to Emily and Joe till at least ten at night and even then they don't want me to go down.

It seems as if either I'm hanging around being available for them but that they're playing with their friends and don't want me, or I've got something going on in the evening, which is when they want my full attention.

SHEILA. The house was full of people. There used to be about ten people at the table and there were too many people coming and going. My children loved it. They feel as at home upstairs as they do here. They are like cousins to the twins. The children feel very secure, they never mind me going out.

I feel the most important time of day, between a mother and child, is at bedtime. You read books and bathe them—it's a cosy time. My kids always have their backs scratched and I ask them what the best thing and the worst thing that happened to them during the day was.

DINAH. My children have got other adults they feel at ease with. I remember, as a child, not having any relationship with any adult, that all adults were just bizarre creatures from a zoo. My mother didn't have any friends; my father wasn't around. My mother was ill and a hermit by nature. I knew nothing about the world, nothing.

SHEILA. The children love having other grown-ups. Alex is marvelous with kids. She is interested in them and likes them, and Dinah does, too. It's very important to have other grown-ups around who appreciate my kids almost as much as I do. Alex and Dinah see their beauty—you know what it's like to be able to talk about your kids with another person who is interested. Yeah, I'm very happy that I live here.

We've had a lot of men living here but there hasn't been one who has really been interested in kids. One guy who lived here didn't even know their names. He asked me once, "What's his name?" after he'd been living here a couple of months—and he thought of himself as a sensitive guy. (Frank is excluded from this remark.)

DINAH. I think it's important to make demands on men relating to kids—on the whole, they don't do it unless demands are put on them by the women. I used to feel so angry. Why should you lie in bed in the mornings while I take the kids to school; why shouldn't you find out what life's like for me—as a woman with kids, as a mother?

When Steve appeared I knew, as a love affair, it was more difficult for Emily to deal with than with the other guys who were just living in the house.

SHEILA.   This place is so small I can't keep anything from my kids. About six months after I split from my husband I started having a love life, and they just took it for granted. I don't want to hide anything from them. It's easier to tell the truth than to tell lies —I don't have a very good memory! Once in a while Michael says to me I'm overdoing it—I don't know where he gets those ideas! But only if it's with a married man, and then he gets a little moralistic.

DINAH.   When Emily and Joe first found Steve in my bed, at first they thought it was their father. And when Emily saw it wasn't she was very shocked. Steve immediately said, "Let's play football," but Emily was suspicious of him for nearly a year. Joe got on very well with him and used to say to me, "I like Steve reading Asterix books more than you because he laughs more," while Emily didn't like him baby-sitting or anything. It was as if she just didn't know how to deal with it. Emily would really like there to be nobody but her and me.

Frank, their father, comes here twice a week. He finds it difficult in a way. At their birthday party he came, but he didn't have any role in the house. Alex and I made the food and Steve rushed round finding a projector for some Laurel and Hardy movies; everyone was busy organizing it, and Frank just sat really. It was difficult for him, he had no role.

They spend every other weekend with Frank but when he visits them here (it's too far for him to take them home just for the evening), he just sits and watches television with them.

SHEILA.   I want them to grow up liberated so I try to share how it is for me; that's the most important thing. I've learnt a lot through the women's liberation movement, and I know the only way women's liberation is going to work is for men to be liberated, too. You can't have one half of the world liberated and the other half not. Most men are just as unliberated as women used to be. I try to bring up the boys to have no role conditioning. They both cook, they each have a night to cook and they have to do the shopping for it. And they have chores to do—sometimes they do the laundry. I know I haven't thought of everything. I wish I knew how to make sure they're not conditioned. We talk about it a lot, joke about it.

POLITICS

DINAH.   When Frank and I first moved here, we were just thinking of living in it in our bourgeois way—room for a housekeeper girl, room for a friend to stay and a laundry room. Everything with labels on—bedroom study—and we thought we'd have a sitting room that the kids could go in and a library where we could read books that the grown-ups would use. And then I began to see that I didn't want to lead a nice bourgeois life and have dinner parties in this rigid social style which exists in middle-class England, which I find empty and deadly. So we thought, yes, we will do things differently. Instead of getting it all painted and decorated by builders we would (a) save money, and (b) learn new skills and generally do things ourselves without a decorator. And I wanted to share with people from the women's group that I was going to.

People then were talking a lot about communal living; we figured we'd share the ground floor, with a big kitchen, and share the sitting room on the ground floor, and then there'd be a two-room flat downstairs. My money was protected by a trust, so I couldn't actually live out my politics by doing anything rash like give it away. There could be a main flat but there couldn't be, according to the terms of the trust, a proper sharing. There was a certain amount of relief when I realized this because that meant it wasn't my fault that I couldn't really share the ownership of the house. But the people I was talking about sharing with in my women's group were aware of the inequalities that would exist and they wanted to share on a more equal basis, and so I didn't share with them. Then I met Sheila, through our kids' being at the same school, who was desperate for a place. When I said, "I want to live communally," she said, "I'll live any way, I need a place so badly." So she moved in and she helped decorate. So then there was Frank and me and Sheila and her two kids and our kids, all living in the house at the same time while her flat downstairs was being decorated. She always thought of the flat downstairs as being her flat, which upset me; and I would very carefully say *the* house, I would try not to use the word my or our or yours, neatly evading the situation. There was another guy about the same time, a German guy who was a friend of a friend and was studying to be a child psychiatrist. He was a very tense, uptight guy who'd lived in a commune in Germany, and so we figured, I figured, ah yes, he would know about communal living so we'd be able to live communally together. And so he moved in, too, and we had absolutely nothing in common and I found that what I was trying to do was to mother him. We cooked these large meals; we made up a schedule so if he didn't come down, I would race upstairs to see how he was. If he wanted food brought up, I wouldn't let him be. I wouldn't let him just do what he wanted to do; I felt if we were living communally, he bloody well ought to eat. I couldn't let him alone. And he didn't stay very long; he left and moved into a flat of his own and good luck to him.

But Sheila, being a very sort of even-tempered person, fitted in with the schedule and was tremendously helpful in the house and painted beautiful murals on my kids' walls and put in a lot of energy. But when it came to October and her flat was finally ready, she moved downstairs to her little cosy private den and could then come up to eat and share a bottle of cheap wine but had her own privacy. And my husband, Frank, was very resentful of this, and I refused to allow that I was resentful of it too. I pretended that I wasn't. The amount of unreality that went on was just amazing.

I'm telling this long story to illustrate how important money and ownership are, because it really is impossible to properly share living space if it is owned by one person. It seems to me that the only people who are working at methods of sharing chores and bills and responsibility, probably the only people who are managing it, are people who are squatting on property they don't own. Because they're in no-man's-land, so the responsibility for actually fixing the place up is equally shared and it's not going to get fixed up unless everybody works on it. It has to be shared because one person doesn't have the power.

Nobody needs eighteen pairs of trousers and nobody needs a skyscraper block or three cars. People's desires are not for what they need; their desires are for fantasies, and people are pursuing their desires and capitalism has got its own momentum boosted by people pursuing fantasies. And often these fantasies are contrary to their interests.

By discussing what kind of a life you were leading in the women's movement, you became aware of ways of changing it. How much they helped me, those early conversations! It's only by becoming aware of what you expect from marriage that you become aware that there is another way of living apart from marriage.

Become aware of what you expect from money: that you expect money to make life easier; that it doesn't unless you know what you're doing with it. That you expect friends to give you some comfort and support, but you don't get it because you don't know how to ask for it. And the ways in which you see friends are so isolated, like inviting people round for dinner. It's a social occasion; you can't talk about what matters to you.

It was through the women's movement that I got close to other women who were sharing the same problems and began to feel that it was up to me to create the life I wanted.

NOW

DINAH. When Sheila and I started sharing the kitchen I felt, at first, an uneasiness, and then I abandoned responsibility for it and thought, It's not my kitchen, it's a shared kitchen, or it's nobody's kitchen; therefore, I don't care about it or take responsibility for it. And then, as our communal thing developed and Alex came and there were more of us, I would come in after a hard day's work and find a nice meal on the table and the food prepared, the kitchen cleaned and the clearing up also done by somebody else because it wasn't my day. I would think, What heaven it is not to have one's own kitchen and to find—it's like being given a gift—to find this meal on the table and people sitting around welcoming you. I felt that by giving up my attachment to control, or that particular part of my space, I was getting back a tremendous amount of nourishment, physical or spiritual, and that was simply because of the structure we had created.

ALEX. Lately we haven't been eating together, which means that if someone wants to see someone, they have to make the effort to go and knock on their door or suggest some coffee or something. I rather like this because we are more specific and immediate in these meetings than when we were all gathered around the dinner table.

The economics have always run very smoothly but Dinah actually owns the house, which means her moods affect the house more. If she's in a bad mood it's somehow a threat to the security, an underlying feeling that she is the deciding factor and could say, "Look, I don't want anybody here—please find someplace else."

DINAH. There's no way that it can't feel like that, because of the practical reality that it is my house, so I can make decisions about it, I can decide to sell it if I want to. When we first started living together I tried to get people to share responsibility for things like unstopping the drains, ringing up somebody to fix the roof if the rain was coming in and fixing the washing machine. And people would do it if I had a fit of hysterics and screamed and yelled and wept and said, "I can't go on, I can't possibly keep this house going—if you lived in a flat you'd still have to clean it or get the drains unstopped." There was a flood downstairs last week and nobody's even thought to ring the plumber. People say, yes, you're right, what's the plumber's telephone number, I'll ring. Or they'd say well, they didn't want to ring the plumber because perhaps they didn't know which plumber I use. I would have to pay, so they didn't know if I wanted to pay the plumber to fix it so they didn't do anything about it. And I was trying to force a sharing on them which was not realistically based because we hadn't made a real commitment to sharing the house. In a way, I haven't committed myself absolutely to having them there. It all seems slightly temporary.

SHEILA. I felt the eating together was very good. I liked to have other grown-ups to talk to instead of talking baby talk.

I once had a boyfriend Dinah couldn't stand, and that made it awkward. But that's the thing in communal living, everybody's got to more or less like each other or it's not going to work.

DINAH. I think everybody needs their own room. But one of the problems here was, if you did settle down in the kitchen with a cup of coffee to have a conversation, you were nearly always interrupted. There was no privacy. And so often I would withdraw, become very remote. Particularly when I'm in the middle of a book, I can't bear to speak to anyone—I put out so much hate and resentment.

This was a stage when there were an awful lot of people living in the house.

Then Emily would always be complaining that she hated the house because there would be nowhere we could be cosy. This was one of the things about being alone—the children could come into the bed in the mornings and read stories, but directly you have a guy there is trouble. My husband never liked the children coming in and waking him up either. I really resented that—I loved them coming into bed and being really cuddly and I resent some sleeping pig of a guy not wanting to be woken up.

SHEILA. It's widened my perception of people. You never see your friends in the same way as you see the people you live with, although some people I haven't got to know at all—they're absolute mysteries to me.

ALEX. I've been living here nearly four years. All the people who live in this house are people who've been through difficult things, who wanted an atmosphere where they could find out who they were and wanted to develop themselves in relation to other people—the sense of extended family really just happened out of the needs of the people who were here.

DINAH. It used to give me fantastic pleasure also to hear people talk about the house, such as somebody deciding to paint the bathroom. But it was mainly the eating that was successful, the pleasure of having different people's ideas about food. There were a lot of vegetarians here and we'd have a lot of vegetarian food. Everybody can cook. I mean people would come and say I've never cooked food in my life, I can't cook; but we'd say well, it's your day. So they'd produce a salad, you know, they'd peel a few carrots and chop some mushrooms. To be offered food is terribly important, and to have the burdens of clearing up and cleaning up shared. It gave everybody a good feeling to produce a nice meal because you only had to do it once a week and, also, it did away with the sort of English social life business—if you wanted someone to come round for dinner, you could ask them round and they'd just join in.

ALEX. I need to know that there is a room, a space I can go to. It's an animal thing—this is my space, my lair.

SHEILA. I like communal eating and cooking but having a private area to work and sleep in. Having the basement here gives me the best of both worlds—I feel welcome whenever I want to join in but I've got my own place here. Sometimes there are too many people upstairs, just bumping into each other.

ALEX. It seems to me that the super advantage we have of living together is that we have to go through things and, at the end, we are still living together. There is a sense of security—that you have the freedom to go through your own changes and your own experiences without becoming isolated, but with definite support. We care about what is happening to each other. To me, it's been the difference between life and death because until I had the experience in my life that there were other people to care about and that other people could care about me, as I am not having to pretend to be something but really allowing myself to find out who I am and living by that, I didn't have anything worth living for. I lived in total isolation in a world where I was involved in "let's pretend" relationships.

LATER

DINAH. Wow, Steve is actually living in the house—it's very nice. He's got his own room, which he doesn't often sleep in. He's taken one of the sofas from downstairs so he could sleep in his room if he wanted to.

I can't get anything to be my own space. It's purely internal difficulty. I can never bring myself to throw anything away, so my room is full of junk. And I also make it serve so many different purposes—I have my women's group meetings in there, my father sometimes comes to stay and he sleeps in there, and I write in there.

I can't call anything my own—that's one of my problems. I can't call my bedroom my own because Steve sleeps there most of the time and when he doesn't, the kids do. Often they go to bed there and get carried up to their own rooms later.

SHEILA. I get very lonely at times because I haven't got a boyfriend at the moment, but I do know that I really like having my freedom and having my choice—not having to compromise and consider other grown-ups' feelings about how I'm going to occupy my time and my evenings.

DINAH. I find it very refreshing with Steve, who has always structured his own life entirely around his own needs. I'm a dependent sort of person. Even when Frank and I were splitting up, I'd listen and wait for him to come home at night—just somehow to fill and structure my life.

I get very dependent on other people's comings and goings. I think somebody who hasn't been married is much less easily conned by women into satisfying their needs, and I hope that someone who has very much structured his own life is less easily conned into doing what I want rather than what he wants and needs.

The idea of getting married again is absolutely unreal.

Steve is prepared to give time to playing with the children and reading to them, to giving them a certain amount of real attention. But when we're all together, he feels usually, Oh, Dinah's here, coping with the kids, so I'll go off and do some work.

I find myself sometimes wishing Steve would do things like watch the television with me and the children, which he hates doing. Sometimes I find myself hankering for that cosy nuclear family thing—which didn't work when I had it, and intellectually I don't think it does work. But I still find myself emotionally trying to recreate it and that frightens me.

When Frank and I were together, and it was him and me and our kids, it was as if nobody was relating to anybody—there were too many crossed lines.

ALEX. Last week my boyfriend went back to his wife and I didn't expect it. And I was hysterically crying when I saw Dinah coming down the road. I leant out of the window and shouted, and she came in and put her arms around me and just let me cry. And that's been terribly important to me—the sense that if I don't get what I need one place, there are people to turn to, there is love and trust.

SHEILA. Living here I feel both accepted and yet not owned. I don't have anyone barking down my throat and telling me what to do. It's been really wonderful to be accepted.

WHERE TO?

Dinah has taken Emily and Joe to live on an ashram in India for a year.

   Sheila might go back to America with her boys for a while.

ALEX. I would be ready now to go back into a relationship with another person in our place. I think I would miss very much not having the other adults and children around that I have here, but something else would happen because I've changed so enormously in the time I've been here.

POSTSCRIPT

Three women and four children formed the heart of this household. Other people have come and gone. Of these, Dinah's former husband, Frank, asked me to let him put in a postscript. And so I asked John, who had lived there with Alex and still lives there on and off, and Steve, who lives there now, to make their comments, too.

JOHN. It's very difficult once the relationship is formed to develop with a lot of people around. There is a communal kitchen and sitting room and so often it was broken up by people coming in whom you had to relate to. It could be very frustrating.

The other evening we'd planned to watch the Dory Previn show on television together—it would have been great to share that—but somebody turned up and wanted Alex's attention, so she was off and for me the evening was spoiled.

It's the same with a meal. There is something intimate about preparing a meal together, going through the whole procedure without interruptions. However, I was married and living in a nuclear family situation and I found it claustrophobic. And the frictions from the relations' living near were more difficult than the commune relationships. It was definitely too narrow, the life with a wife and child and a small flat. I need other people. I think it is a battle to find the time to be alone with the woman you love and yet to see other people freely.

At first I found it difficult living with children who weren't mine. I often felt very guilty when I was playing with them because I was with them when I should have been with my own son. I used to get very upset.

I enjoyed it when we all went out together. Once we all went to the park together and played, children with grown-ups, doing handstands, throwing a ball about. Another time they'd mown the heath and made this big haystack, and we went up there and did tumbling about in the hay with the kids and ended up lying in the warm hay together as it got dark. It was a very special feeling, having the whole household together. I felt very close, that they were all there for me.

I was brought up in a traditional family life and here was such a totally different experience for me. I'd before only thought people could be intimate with their blood relations; now I see they can be far closer and more supportive to the people they choose to live with.

FRANK. Dinah and I bought the house and moved into it four and a half years ago, at a time when she was intensely involved in women's lib and I was an ardent supporter of it. For ideological and emotional reasons we decided to turn the house into a sort of commune.

This decision led us into dimly foreseen complications, arising from the fact that we owned the house and were the only sexually cohabiting couple in it. Thus, the members of our sort of commune were, in practical reality, tenants and, in an emotional reality, members of our family, drawn into the vortex of our marriage. This may be a matter of dispute but if they joined anything, it was a marriage, not a commune; and it was a marriage that rapidly disintegrated. Two years after we moved into the house Dinah and I separated and, by mutual agreement, I moved out.

In reading the interviews I get the impression that the household now is a cosy, warm and pleasant place. It wasn't such for me when I was there during the two most agonizing years of my life, in which the three women all played their parts. I don't blame them for my agony, but they were involved in it; and knowing as I do the unspoken history of the household, I regard what they say with some cynicism—including what Dinah says about the way I was with my children.

I have, in fact, just written a book about my marriage and the impact on it of the women's movement, in which I deal in some detail with this household. No doubt when all three women read it they too will find passages that do not please them. That can hardly be helped. What I am intent on saying here is that there is much more to this household than meets the eye.

STEVE. I came here, not because I wanted a place to live, but because I wanted to be with Dinah. And now she's gone to India. Although the people living here are fine, they don't really want to spend a lot of time together—though Alex suggested we should have a group together, but somehow I don't feel it's going to happen.

I got a lot from living with the children. I found, with Joe and Emily, I really enjoyed being with them. There were times when Dinah was away that I took responsibility for them, but most of the time it wasn't as if I was in any way pretending to be a parent to them—I just played with them when I felt like it. Joe and I had a great thing about reading Asterix books together.

Early on there was definitely a period of hostility. I don't think I've ever felt such strong jealousy for many years as I did between Dinah's daughter and me. There was all this bit from Emily that she wanted to sleep in Dinah's bed and why couldn't she spend all night there, which Dinah found quite hard to deal with. Then gradually the situation eased.

I think having a relationship with a woman living with children does have difficulties, and it's taken me a long time to realize you can't have the same sort of relationship as you can if there's just the two of you. If there's just two of you, all your emotional problems and strengths flow into each other and you get a very intense inward relationship. And I found, with Dinah, I just had to accept the fact that there was a lot of time when she was busy with the kids.

In the last year she's consciously tried to give them a lot of attention because she really wanted to, and because of the separation from their father. Early on she found it difficult to be very involved with them, which is one of the reasons she's gone to India—to have an adventure with them.

There was something that definitely appealed to me about having a family suddenly presented to me. There was something about having a relationship with a woman who is a mother that's a whole dimension that isn't there with a woman without children. The two things are different. The relationship with a woman who is very involved with her children isn't the same as having a relationship with a single woman, and maybe if you try and pretend it's the same, it's going to bust.

I think living in a commune was definitely an advantage—in fact, I've never lived à deux. A lot of my energy and my life were going into Tai Chi, and so, in a way, Dinah having the kids and me having my studies and both of us being a part of this commune, did lead to quite a free situation and a good balance. The Tai Chi was extremely demanding, so there was a polarity in the situation.

I remember, quite early on, the children went away for the weekend and I said to Dinah, "Fantastic, you can have all this time to yourself," and Dinah felt suddenly totally stranded and lost without them.

I feel her going to India for a year means I don't know what will happen between us, but it also means I've time to miss her, to reflect and perhaps get myself more together.

I simply paid rent for the room and my part of the housekeeping, like everyone else, so Dinah and I never had any financial hassles. I don't want to take any responsibility for her house— I've got my own house anyway—and I don't want all the "married" dealings that go on between people. And the same with the kids. They're Dinah's kids and when I'm around I love to see them and play with them, but I don't want to act out or take over responsibility for them, and Dinah feels the same. We talk about them a lot but, finally, they are her responsibility.

One of the things that makes living with Dinah so easy is I don't feel, in any way, she's neurotic. It isn't as if she's trying to cling to things or trying to create some careful form of shelter or protection. She lives her mad life but she doesn't expect anyone else to take responsibility for her. I like that and it makes me feel quite free myself.

I do feel it is a burden on Dinah that she owns the house. In some ways, now she isn't here and we all pay rent, it is a situation of more equal responsibility.

I like this household an awful lot. I feel I could have lived here and flourished.

The ownership problem still loomed large—a shared mortgage seems the only way round this one. But I envied the living together of women, particularly women involved in the arts. Perhaps it is romantic of me to imagine that there was something of the prewar Paris feeling about that kitchen—ideas flitting between them, their close involvement in other art forms I am so out of touch with. And I do get something very different through close contact with women, which I can't get through men.

Just because I'm a mother I'm not going to do certain things that are expected of me, and I tell my kids that. Sometimes I get paranoid that society is going to interpret my actions as psychically unsound. I sleep with women, I go to London and leave my children with people, I explore different ways of life. I could be diagnosed as mad and have my children taken away.

12. BISEXUAL PARENT: JACKIE

Jackie is exotic.

One of my reasons for doing this book was that I wanted to find out how other people were finding satisfaction in their domestic lives. I think I've learned most from Jackie. She is astonishingly courageous and open, so much so that for a split second I felt I had to protect my seventeen-year-old son from meeting her—and thereby revealed yet another of my double standards: "It's all right for me, but one must protect the children from bisexuality and freedom."

She is also immensely creative. She is a driving force in Sister Show, and has made films and written for various papers, includ-

ing Spare Rib. *She writes poetry and is hoping to have a book of poems published.*

I spent some happy times, sitting on the floor of her room by the fire, talking. And when she came to my house it suddenly seemed stiff and formal—there was too much furniture and too many objects. How can you be free with a whole lot of stuff to look after?

She lives on the top floor of a small row house in Bristol with her sons, Dominic, eleven, and Jason, eight, who both go to the free school. John, her husband, lives on the ground floor. **"**

WHERE FROM?

JACKIE.   This house, the home John and I had, was the first home I'd had since I was eleven years old. My mother had multiple sclerosis and was too ill to look after us, and we were fostered out. So this home meant an awful lot to me. It was, perhaps, harder for me to break it than it might have been for other women, but I couldn't stand what John was expecting of me without going mad!

Three or four years before we split, we lived a fairly typical married life. John worked, I had the babies and looked after the home. I enjoyed making the home. I decorated it. It was exciting, there was a certain amount of team work and we pulled together. It worked best in the early years, when it was a struggle, when there were more things to strive for. From time to time I wanted more—I was bored—but on the whole I liked it and we had lots of friends. I was happy.

That home had been built with love. We led a social life in couples—other arty, trendy couples we had met at art school. This was in the sixties. We were young married people getting a bit of money. We rated. We had a home and trendy kids' names. We were very much of the sixties—even John being a hairdresser was very trendy. The women in all these couples didn't demand too much in their own right; they were happy to be married and to give dinner parties and meet other people doing quite creative things. We moved in couples, we fitted in with the scheme of things. Young couples. Young children. It was a social scene—we gossiped a lot.

Then the dogs came. First there was one. These precious Yorkshire terriers. They represented John's divine right to do as he wished in this house because he was the man and he paid for it, and my inability to assert that same right. So there I was, seeing these dogs getting more and more of my space. They weren't house-trained and I was expected to clean up after them. And they'd yap and I had to look after them all day, to stop them running out into the road. The dogs led to a lot of rows and fighting and neither of us giving in. I suppose that overflowed into our sexual relationship; the situation was unfair. The dogs, although it is laughable, were a threat to our relationship. They led John away from me—he became deeply involved with them, more interested in them than me. One day I asked him, "How do you think it feels, John, to be second in your life to something with fur and four legs?" He said, "You're not, dear. I have five dogs, you're sixth." So it affected our sexual relationship. I was making love with the man who was causing me misery. I was feeling resentful yet wanting us to be O.K., but also feeling he didn't really want me.

I remember fancying a man at a party, and I danced with him and then I felt so guilty—so guilty about fancying another man and I was miles from following it through. That shows how brainwashed I was—this "faithful to the marriage bed" bit—or perhaps how settled I was.

Now I don't see those same people. It's almost as if you're on your own. You see other people on their own; you don't see couples much.

But anyway, I got fed up with that couple thing. John and I both competed about who could be the most amusing. We were an amusing couple; we mocked marriage sometimes, and the dogs

—a way of getting by. I was a creation of John's to an extent. He did my hair, he chose and bought me clothes; I looked good. He selected things for me—out of affection, to give and get pleasure from it; he would like people to like his creation as long as it remained his. That fell apart when I started to do my own things. I got less. Now he laughs at me and what I wear.

I couldn't leave my kids permanently. I did think about it but I realized I was attached to them at gut level. I discovered it by going away. I had a lot to work out for myself at that time. John's friend moved in while I was away. This was a terrible blow because I had never brought anyone into the home; and even though both of us had lovers, the home was for me a base—it was the family—I would never have brought someone in to live with me. It freaked me because I wasn't consulted in any way, and the inequality freaked me. I was expected to take it without a murmur. I remember feeling very stunned. I lived for a year in a three situation, but it was too difficult to take. I got more and more depressed. I minded John and his friends being together much more than I thought I would, though John and I weren't by then sleeping together. I hated him moving the kids' stuff out of the front room. It was my home. I minded a lot but I was so screwed up I couldn't say anything.

I was jealous and I was resentful, because he would never have allowed me to do it. And that's what I was striving for, that's what all my arguments were about, equality. And then we had this famous conversation that I made into a sketch in the show with one of my best "sisters" playing John. I said to him, "Why don't you treat me like you treat your friend, with the same consideration?" It was galling to me to see this person treated with preference in my own territory. He would say, "My friend wants the front room tidy—take the kids' toys out." He strove after a kind of status symbol of the perfectly tidy home untouched by kids.

I tried to tell John. I said, "Did you realize how shocked and shattered I was by you moving your friend in?" I asked him what I did wrong in the marriage. He said, "You didn't keep the place clean and dusted." So I said, "Yes, but what did I actually do that was hurtful to you?" And he said quite simply, "You didn't look after me." I asked, "Was the dust on the shelves the reason you began to hate me?" He said, "You didn't do your job, Jackie, you were lazy." So, as some movie star once said, "My husband and I had a weird and wonderful relationship . . . he was weird and I was wonderful!"

NOW

It's no good men thinking they can be the kingpins in my life because they can't. I've had to go from one identity to another in this street; I was here as a wife and mother of two nice children and I've had to come away from that. It represented to me the straight world—all my conditioning, my parents—and that is a part of me, too. Now I'm relating with Sue, who is only twenty, and the straight world would be horrified by me carrying on a sexual relationship with a young girl of twenty. Just because I'm a mother I'm not going to do certain things that are expected of me, and I tell my kids that. Sometimes I get paranoid that society is going to interpret my actions as psychically unsound. I sleep with women, I go to London and leave my children with people, I explore different ways of life. I could be diagnosed as mad and have my children taken away.

I've come to terms with the chores of having children. Sometimes I do it, sometimes they do it and if someone is here with me, like Sue for instance, then she'll do part of the work, too. She's only twenty but I never want to play the mother to her. There may be aspects of that in the nature of the relationship; I feel I want a mother myself sometimes.

Territorially, it's my flat still. Sue has a room in a house near here but she sleeps here most nights. I don't know if I want to live with anyone in a tight couple situation. We have quite a domestic scene; we often cook if we feel like it, and she does things with the kids. It's definitely my territory but she spends a lot of time here. But I want freedom in the relationship so we can spend time alone or with other people.

It's the freedom to say no. With John the expectations he had of me were so set. Even if I did say, "Couldn't you sometimes put the kids to bed?" the answer would be, "No, that's your job." And I didn't have that sort of freedom.

I find less and less that I need to hide things from people—it's such a luxury to be open. When I was with John, there were things I was loath to reveal because his reaction would be negative—that held quite a lot back. Now I enjoy the freedom of saying whatever I have to say and not minding if someone doesn't like it, or the freedom of cuddling a woman in front of a man. I'd like to be less aware of John just underneath. Perhaps that's because I'm still tied up with him—we share the bathroom. And I still find resistance emotionally to John's friend—he did a take-over and it was my home, although this person is a nice person.

My relationships with other women have been relationships for the physical and emotional content but never the sharing of a life-style. In the whole issue of carving out a lifestyle with another woman there's still something in me that wants a balance. If I've been with a woman for a condensed amount of time—just mud-dling along together, having an easy time—then after a while I'll find myself hoping one of my men friends will come along. It's something male—the other polarity perhaps.

I did ask John the other day if he could ever live with me again and he said, "No," and I said, "Why? I understand all about men and it's all right!" And he said no, he couldn't go through the fighting. In a funny way it was a relief—it was definite, I knew where I was. But I also felt sad—the closing of a door.

Because he isn't supporting me or the kids, I have to live on Social Security. John says to me, "You're a parasite, why don't you get out to work?"

I miss some of the nice things—John's got most of the nice

things in his half of the house. I looked around for somewhere else to live but on the sort of money I would have, it would have been a really grungy place, and I didn't think I could cope with putting the kids through too much mess.

The kids know we've got no money. My responsibility is to give them the awareness of what is happening in the world. It bugs me that John's got a color television and I've got a black-and-white one. And he won't let the children watch his unless he's in, in case they mess up his flat. But I accept it and I think they do—in fact, Dominic says, "I sort of can't relax down there." That was something I got from moving into relationships with women—that I don't interfere with John, that he can live how he wants and that I mustn't be concerned with it. Let him get on with his own life; I don't want to live like that but that's his business. I've got the kids—he doesn't want to involve himself with them practically.

John used to help if I was doing things that fitted in. He used to lay it on me—"I keep you. Therefore you will do the cleaning and that's what I keep you for." So I decided, I don't want that laid on me so I won't take money from you. So when I left for a few months I got on Social Security—now the State keeps me and the kids because he doesn't.

I think the people I go towards are into love of life—of nature and people and the world—in a realistic way. You've got to be tough as well. I don't hanker after a lot of heavy products—I don't need a fancy kitchen. Most of my spare money goes on traveling—I go to London every two or three weeks, mostly to see people or organize work.

CHILDREN

I'm finding living alone a luxury. I'd like to be still more alone sometimes, but how do I get to be alone when I've got kids? I try to incorporate the kids in things—I can talk about anything in front of them. I'd be careful about intimate sexual things but I wouldn't have to hide the actual relationships.

Since I split with John, I've had less space and the kids around me more. A different lifestyle because before, friends of mine couldn't come and visit that easily because John was there doing the husband thing. The kids have joined in the relationships I've been having and in some ways that's been good. But there comes a point when I don't want them around and then I say, "You must go to bed," or "You must go to your rooms." Or I go out—I go out a lot and they stay at home or go out. I was determined to cling onto a certain amount of freedom so Dominic and Jason have had to accept that I'll go out or I'll go away when I want to. They stay in other people's houses a lot, or their friends come here— there is a merry-go-round of kids.

I'm going away this weekend and I asked Dominic if he'd like to stay in the flat with a friend and look after himself. And he thought that was fabulous—he was delighted—and Jason is going to stay with someone else. I think a gift that I can give my kids is the ability to look after themselves when they go out into the world.

They know an awful lot about me and I don't think it has harmed them to see I'm not infallible. I think if you show your kids your reality in all its forms, then they are secure because there is something there, something tangible. It's when you don't that they're insecure. They can deal with the worst things in the world if they're true.

SEX AND LOVE

I'm beginning to think that I've sorted out my emotions as far as John is concerned, that I can't completely get him out of my hair.

I accept that now—I've had nearly half my life with him and therefore I accept our relationship as ongoing.

Maybe my bisexuality manifested itself because I wanted to keep the home and I didn't want to set up a rival relationship to John. A dual process, outside-inside. Having relationships with women was tied up with exploring myself. It took me out of the domestic scene, of being a wife. It was exploring my identity as myself as an artist. It was tied up with getting into the women's movement in the very early days, about nineteen seventy. Then relationships with women sprung up. I was pretty freaked-out when I realized this woman, also the mother of children, was turning me on—that was completely uncharted landscape. I knew where I was with men, but this was something else and it had a lot of impact on me emotionally. It also meant I was exploring an identity that was nothing to do with any man; it was to do with me. It was a big chunk of making a stand. Gay lib wasn't around then—there was nobody to talk to at all.

I told John about it and he said, "It won't do you any good in the long run—it will make you unhappy." She and I were both very freaked-out; we neither of us quite knew what had happened and we wouldn't talk about it very much.

Then I went on into another relationship with a woman, and by that time gay lib had started and I wasn't groping about so much and it was a much stronger scene. I had a lot of gay friends, women and men.

The problem between John and me comes from the fact that my lifestyle is open—I don't really care about middle-class hang-ups any more. I don't lead my life according to any expectations from the outside that are put on me. I do what I want to do. It hasn't always been easy, but my identity now, as a woman, includes having relationships with women. I'm living in a society where the white heterosexual male is the most desirable thing to be, and it is he who dictates the terms. And if you aren't one, you should at least have one—that is, a husband—and in these terms I'm completely at the bottom rung of the ladder.

I get a lot of support from my close friendships with women.

My relationship with Sue I don't see as permanent necessarily. It is strong and deep. I'm not looking for a permanent relationship, more for emotional stability. It could be, who knows? I feel that the marriage hasn't gone altogether and that I don't want to enter into another similar relationship. I feel the marriage roles and expectations destroyed our relationship to an extent. I am not saying a relationship in marriage cannot work. And two people seems a good number. I respect other people's relationships. It's lovely to see, for instance, an old couple who have been married sixty years, who have grown together. It's when people are forced to remain together—when person A is dependent on person B for identity, security—a trap, that can be bad.

A lot of people make a lot of money out of married couples—consumerism. A lot of commodities which promise to make a happy home—things people don't need, nothing to do with love, nothing to do with the relationship—and they become replacements. It's a con—the relationship stays empty. This is not a socialist-Marxist argument here particularly. I am not yelling change society, the rotten capitalist bastards, all that, or saying you shouldn't have because I have not. I am looking at potential dangers of taking refuge in the material and neglecting emotional. I like material things too, beautiful things. We need our props, dear! But we have an energy crisis. What *do* we need? What's our responsibility to the world? What's mine? Perhaps I find my relationships with women important because I can be myself. I have my own identity—there are no roles set up by society for two women. It's less secure in many ways but it's terrifically free. There aren't any expectations from outside on that relationship, it's for itself.

I don't want a pair-bond situation that would be a couple parodying the married situation. I don't want that with a woman. The very essence for me is relating with a woman as an equal, relating in a free way. Sue is a woman with whom I am having a physical and emotional relationship. It's a gay relationship in that it is being emotionally and physically explored, but there are no roles set. They are interchangeable as needs arise. And it's important that she should be free to explore where she wants to, and be honest with me.

I feel jealousy, but I'm working hard to get over and above feeling jealousy. I'm working hard on trying to love somebody absolutely for herself and accepting what she does and not interpreting it in terms of my own security. As far as John is concerned, I don't agree with the way he lives, but I see now he must be free to do what he wants and see things his way, and I needn't identify and react to him in an angry way. I know now, I have learnt now that you can only change yourself; you can only ultimately learn about yourself through relating. If you feel negative feelings, they are in you to be dealt with, learned from; they are not put there by the other person, really, but experienced through relating with them. Take it inward, not outward, to state or society or whatever. There's always something or somebody to spit venom at if that's what you have to do. I have been growing towards changing my negativity into other energy, dealing with anger in myself. I see now that my fights with John were that I wanted him to change; it was a process that took time to see. I got stronger and weaker, I got out anger through the fights; perhaps I was testing myself. I accept him now, much much more.

One thing I find very good about relating to Sue and other women is that we can talk about what's happening between us all the time—I feel this is conducive to the relationship being solid. I can say to her, "I want space, I can't see you for a few days," and that's fine because she's got a room of her own. I go there sometimes; I like it. Once I went at six thirty in the morning to find her. I crept in the back way and got into bed with her. I was so pleased she was there. We had had a row. So it's not really about a man or a woman but a relationship, a trip . . .

I don't know who would suit me in that mate kind of way. There is no right person. Perhaps it would have to be a man who accepts my terms or who has carved out his own definition of himself or who is bisexual. Anyway, these are thoughts and theories.

I'm not into having physical or, particularly, emotional relationships with a lot of people—I just haven't got the time to go in for a lot of heavy sexual and emotional things.

I'm not disinterested in men sexually, but my ongoing relationships with men are linked with my creativity.

I've discovered, since we first spoke a year ago, that it is women who have taken up a lot of my time. Not exclusively—there are my kids who are both boys. It's women I am with, want to be with; men are in my life if they acept that—which sorts things out pretty quickly—or if they are gay! It's not an issue like a man-woman war, just about people. Some men are good at doing things I can't do, or have no pull to doing—"stereotypical" things. So what? They have a different culture. I don't want to be a man; I love being a woman on my own terms. I got a man to lay my kitchen floor tiles. I could have done it but he was good and he was available and I wanted to do other things. Radical lesbians who are carving out a new lifestyle without men? Right on. New women, new concept of women being formed by the living of it —we're evolving. I think the gay thing could be an evolutionary balance thing. I am not angry at men anymore, I just get on with my life. My creativity and time is a woman's statement. I am putting it up to be seen in performance, in shows, taking risks; I cannot wait, there is no choice. I bring everything I can to bear on the situation in which the statement is being made—writing, moving, photos, sounds, film, bodies, clothes, whatever seems relevant. I want to see a balance, the growing of a woman's culture, their own.

I haven't been long enough out of the marriage to be sure of what I want. I don't want to replace the marriage with another marriage-type situation. I'm still exploring. I'm not looking for permanence. I want emotional security. That's important—I don't want to float into a new person every three weeks. I do have expectations from my relationships—of honesty, of laughter, of fantasy, of surprises, of silk handkerchiefs for tears and of silence. I want to be anyone I want to be, who I am from moment to moment.

POLITICS

I see the gay thing as part of my search for my own identity. It's me as a woman carrying out things for myself, doing my own work, my own creativity. My politics are my creativity. Sexuality has been the issue for me—that we should be free as people.

We had a bit of money in the sixties. It was perhaps a commercial mentality—pretty sheets and pretty shoes. I miss that but I don't crave it; I've changed. It's all part of change: my diet, acupuncture, meditation and influences from certain people, being with good energy and making good energy aid learning.

Perhaps we've all got to live in a much simpler way. We've got to be less greedy and that's my contribution. And the visual thing—that's my training, that's my awareness. I am seduced by nice-looking things, if you like, but my lifestyle is the result of an ideology, doing what feels right. We've all got to be much more responsible about what we use and what we need and waste —and really we don't need lots of things to have a nice life, and I'd like to give my children that which they're getting. I do not see the world as a bad place except if things are bad in me. I like life; life can be exciting with or without a lot of things! Or it can be reaching for the suicide pills.

THE FUTURE

When I say the marriage has not quite gone, perhaps I am still aware of that way of life with someone else, perhaps I might like to replace the marriage with someone else. It's just a wonder— I'm not troubled about it. I spoke to a man I've known for ages;

his marriage went years ago, he's been free, alone and in affairs. "Nothing's easy," we were saying, so I proposed to him and we both laughed and laughed but we knew what we meant.

I feel at a point where that's very exciting because I can see that it is possible to do all the things that I've dreamed about or dream about. I suddenly say, Why not? There's less and less holding me back. Perhaps, the more you carve out, the more you can see to do, and I don't want anybody to take that away from me. That's why I'm hesitant about another pair-bond. It's too exciting, it's too new, this feeling of being in charge of my own life, of thinking, Yes, of course I can do that new book or new project. It's just a matter of fitting it in, finding a way around the difficulties. It doesn't exclude relationships but it's finally an independence, a belonging to myself.

I think Jackie's relationship to money is liberating. She always dresses exotically. Last time I saw her she was wearing a khaki coverall, a fox-fur cape, a knitted hat and high, rope-soled shoes —"All from the jumble sales, darling."

She appears to live on nothing, yet she is never drab or crushed. Why? She doesn't seem to expect the things I expect—a centrally heated house, a drink every night and much more. She hitches about; she's as thin as a rake but claims she never goes hungry.

"I just don't think money," she says. "After all, if you've got none to spend, you can't spend any." Whereas I think money all the time, have plenty and yet am anxious about it. Sometimes I feel it's overwhelmingly important to be able to buy just what I want when I want and that's what freedom is. But meeting Jackie made me feel that this was a problem in me (and others), that freedom is something else, which she has discovered.

13. WHAT I LEARNED

I'd like to try to say what I've learned from the year I've spent making this book.

Marriage. *It has become clear to me that I am against marriage and the nuclear family, not because there is necessarily a lack of love, but because it is a "stuck" situation. In the nuclear family the control patterns get stuck—everybody is controlling each other. The dutiful husband is as much a prisoner as is the dominating wife. The dominating father as much as the dutiful daughter.*

Nobody can invent a lifestyle that continues to be satisfying. Everything has to be reinvented all the time. In marriage, you are legally frozen into a certain position. Very few marriages leave room for change. What landscape doesn't grow stale seen every day above a kitchen sink heavy with expectations. Expectations for women—to be there, to make a home and, what's more, a bright, warm, clean, cheerful home. And for men—to be elegant superearners, strong and sexy. And for children—to be clean, healthy, exam-passers.

The only way I can be in touch with my own energy is by feeling responsible for my own life. Outside control breeds inertia—I want to stay in bed. Ideally, in the commune structure, everybody is under their own control, except for communal activities such as cooking and cleaning, which are communally controlled. Nobody has more power than anybody else. This, for me, was the first and most important discovery about communes.

Children. *When Gem, my eight-year-old son, produced a shoe box that he'd been keeping under his bed for a year, with a one-armed doll with pointed tits (given to him by his friend Charlotte), he said, "This is a secret; don't tell anyone because they'll call me sissy." We went and bought her a frilly white blouse at a market and he said, "Why, when boys play with Action Man, don't they call them sissies?" A good comment and I thought how young the mothering instinct is quenched in little boys. Why shouldn't they be encouraged to play with dolls? Wouldn't they grow up more naturally towards fatherhood?*

In Leeds the kids are growing up free of roles because they are being directly cared for by men as much as by women. I feel the Leeds parents are freer to enjoy their children because the anxiety and the responsibility are spread between eleven. There is more support when there are problems—it isn't all "your fault"—more open discussion; more grown-up life, such as sitting up for spaghetti with garlic sauce, or Misha wandering round the house at seventeen months visiting the different rooms—Annie's with the delicate home-made lampshade or Albert's, full of electronic bits and pieces. There, nobody feels the pressure to relate or show love to the child—which is so unlike the mother who is in an anguish of guilt about the love she cannot (that day) feel.

Another thing that occurred to me: having twenty-four-hour care or responsibility for a child does not necessarily mean the mother (or father) is bored. Just as often he or she becomes obsessed by that child, so that his or her dreams and waking thoughts are totally invaded by the youngster. (I had a friend who dreamed often of her year-old child shitting—it was her most pleasurable dream.) In the end, neither mother nor child has any separate identity.

In the commune situation there are other adults around, mending punctures, cooking rice, reading books about the Middle East. A lot will be absorbed without their noticing. The choice of interests widens, the choice of a way of life—variety, endless possibilities. The Leeds children are spirited. They are looked after with enthusiasm; the adults are not trapped by duty.

Dominic, Jackie's son, is also a special child. He is lively and companionable, and nothing shocks him. He is happy to organize his own life. There are plenty of places to go and people to see and, as Jackie says, what they haven't got they improvise. Dominic and his brother Jason (who never got photographed because he was out and about, busy all weekend with friends) are not neglected because she is willing to share so much with them, her thoughts, her experience. And yet basically, she leaves them free. "Their lives belong to them." When she needs to go away, she goes. So it isn't necessarily the commune situation that allows a child to develop as an independent creature—a parent can do it. Yet even Jackie relies on the "merry-go-round" of kids in Bristol to extend their lives—Dominic and Jason have access to a lot of houses.

There is a certain emotional muscularity to be won from dealing with children. It is a struggle and sometimes it seems a struggle with no letups, as it must have sometimes seemed to David, bringing up Jonathan. Yet, with experiment and openness and quite a bit of risk—which many of us don't feel prepared to take— children will grow into self-determining people who don't need our constant care and attention, who will be both interested in and interesting to us.

Jackie has given her children self-reliance, which is so different from neglect. The same is true of Sue's children in Brighton, and the Leeds toddlers are aimed in this direction. This is what I learned about children: the more freedom you give them, the more you share with them the things you genuinely love, the less you do for them the things they can do for themselves, the more they flourish.

•

I want to try to say something about myself, how I'm living now and what I hope for from my domestic situation.

Halfway through writing the book, still living with Dan, I got sterilized. I realized not only that I did not want any more children but also, and perhaps more significantly, I didn't want to be in another coparent relationship. I wanted to have a free relationship which depended on nothing more than the desire to spend time and emotion, and which could be broken with a minimum of practical inconvenience. It seems a biologically insoluble problem—what to do about the shared child when the shared life is no longer wanted. Someone is almost certainly, for geographical if for no other reasons, going to forgo the luxury of living with his or her child.

The other big event was I went away with Dan for two and a half months, taking my three children and his four, to camp in the Pyrenees. I discovered a real delight in exploring the world with my kids. How boring the parent-at-home role can be—getting them to school and to the dentist, getting them to clear up. In the mountains it was discovering a deep pool in the river to swim in, showing Reuben and Jem how to climb rocks, listening to Roc playing his sopranino. Once we all swam and waded two miles down a river to a village. . . . That was a magic day. We need adventures with our children where the situations are new to us as well—we're in it together. That's why Dinah has gone to India with Joe and Emily.

My relationships with Dan's children were far more difficult, the most difficult thing being jealousy. I was jealous of them; they were jealous of me; my children were jealous of Dan and (I boldly speak for him) he was jealous of them; and all the children were jealous of each other. In spite of that, I like them (but then they're lovely kids, which is why I'm so jealous of them).

I realized that the desire of a child for a home is not only a desire for identity and security but also the desire for independence. It is simpler with a settled base to make independent relationships and to rendezvous with the outside world.

I found group living difficult in another way as well—the effort to remain detached, not to be invaded by the others' moods, "You may be bored but I'm feeling marvelous and I'm going to have a lovely day." There was so much going on within the group that I found it almost impossible to have freedom of spirit. Often my energy got low. I found it hard to do things by myself, perhaps, finally, to see myself as a separate person. I was over-aware of everyone else's needs—the typical trap for a woman, "the emotional heart of every house."

In whatever situation I live, I feel absolutely certain that I need a separate room or tent, however small, completely to my-self, that smells of me and is inhabited by my thoughts and things.

Food. *I want to say something about food because it has often been a problem for me when I've felt it my duty to feed the men and children around me. Now that my youngest child is eight I cook if I feel like it, which is about once or twice a week. Other-wise they feed themselves.*

I was in a French brasserie the other day and I thought how ideal the food was there, how I'd like my kitchen to be like a bras-serie. Beer in the refrigerator, eggs, fresh bread, mustard, toma-toes, good coffee, fruit. We don't need more elaborate meals than this. If sometimes we feel like cooking them, that's great.

Visiting Brighton just lately, I noticed a beautiful plate rack made by Zapp of bamboo. It sloped down out over the sink. David was cursing it, as four plates he had put in had crashed to the floor. "Ah," said Sue, "it's a Zen plate rack, you have to take care."

I feel life at Murren presented endless possibilities for im-provisation—a child spent all day taking a rusty broken bicycle to pieces, cleaning it and rebuilding it. Martin tried out different kinds of buildings, huts and towers for the children. The successful ones could be later used at work.

In Brighton, the house is furnished (and heated, by abandoned wood) from the local dump, and quite magnificently furnished at that. In Leeds, the women had banded together and formed a theater group. In Ramsgate, they'd invented the Dream Book.

The Unanswered Question, for me, is, Do most of us need a passionate central relationship? And, if so, can this be part of a communal existence?

My need for comforting and care is enormous. I want to live in a way that affords closeness of contact, physical and mental. How wide can I spread this? How many people can I be open with? I equally need change and adventure.

Most "couple" relationships don't yield to our inner longings for drama and unpredicted events in our lives. As we get older, creativity is stifled and burned on the altar of maturity and security. We are not free to own our own experience, and when we do, we feel guilty. Coupledom often works against our deep longings to yield—to give way—to fears, to excitement, to wildness . . .

In the commune situation, such as at Brighton and Leeds, one could hope to find support—there is no partner to be threatened, no marriage to be broken up by a distressful or joyous adventure. There are only other individuals struggling to be free, too.

Dan and I have, over the last year, become more aware of these traps. We struggle to maintain a free relationship and to evolve separate nonrole links with each of the children. We fight a lot. Jealousy is still an enormous problem.

I hope to become more open.

There is no right way or wrong way to live; there is only what you want. I want to risk having what I want.

My life belongs to me. **99**

Date Due